everyday
barbecue

PaRragon

Bath New York Singapore Hong Kong Cologne Delhi Melbourne

This edition published by Parragon in 2009

Parragon
Queen Street House
4 Queen Street
Bath
BA1 1HE, UK

Copyright © Parragon Books Ltd 2008
Cover design by Talking Design
Designed by Terry Jeavons & Company
Additional text written by Linda Doeser

ISBN 978-1-4075-5622-2

Printed in China

Notes for the Reader
This book uses both metric and imperial measurements. Follow the same units of measurement throughout; do not mix metric and imperial. All spoon measurements are level: teaspoons are assumed to be 5 ml, and tablespoons are assumed to be 15 ml. Unless otherwise stated, milk is assumed to be full fat, eggs and individual vegetables are medium, and pepper is freshly ground black pepper.

The times given are an approximate guide only. Preparation times differ according to the techniques used by different people and the cooking times may also vary from those given. Optional ingredients, variations or serving suggestions have not been included in the calculations.

Recipes using raw or very lightly cooked eggs should be avoided by infants, the elderly, pregnant women, convalescents and anyone suffering from an illness. Pregnant and breastfeeding women are advised to avoid eating peanuts and peanut products. Sufferers from nut allergies should be aware that some of the ready-made ingredients used in the recipes in this book may contain nuts. Always check the packaging before use.

everyday
barbecue

introduction

Eating outdoors is always fun and there's something especially appetizing about food cooked on a barbecue. Everyone enjoys themselves – old and young, family and friends, even the cook – and

there are great dishes to suit all tastes and budgets. In fact, the variety of barbecue dishes and the range of ingredients are surprising – from traditional burgers, steak and ribs to fabulous whole fish, butterflied poultry, vegetable parcels and even fruity desserts. You can keep things really simple with cheeseburgers, a green salad and ready-made dressing or push the boat out with a choice of marinated meats,

chargrilled vegetables, rice salad and home-made salsas, finishing triumphantly with fruit kebabs. One of the best things is that however much preparation you want to undertake, it's all done in advance.

Safety is important but it's mostly a matter of common sense. Follow the manufacturer's instructions for positioning, lighting, using and cleaning your barbecue. If using charcoal, remember to light it well in advance and have a bucket of water and/or sand nearby just in case. Make sure somebody is responsible for keeping an eye on any children and pets and never leave a lighted barbecue unattended. Don't take raw food outdoors until you're ready to start cooking and keep it covered. Keep sauces and dressings cool, especially if, like mayonnaise, they contain raw eggs. Use separate tools for raw and cooked meat and check that poultry and pork in particular are thoroughly cooked. Pierce the thickest

part with the point of a sharp knife and, if there's any trace of pink or red in the juices, cook the meat for a little longer and check again. Drain off marinades before putting meat or fish on the grill to avoid flare-up and if you're going to use a marinade as a sauce, make sure you bring it to the boil first.

best burgers

It's hard to imagine a barbecue without burgers and, once you've tasted the home-made variety, you'll always include them in future. Not only is the flavour so much better than shop-bought burgers, but there are no additives and you know exactly what has gone into the mix, so you can easily control the size and the quantities of fat and salt. What's more, a barbecue is for grilling, not frying, so all of a sudden this demon junk food becomes a fully paid-up member of the healthy diet club.

The burger has come a long way from its humble beginnings among German immigrants to the United States and you will be amazed at the variety and range of recipes. You can use all kinds of meat, from traditional minced steak to duck, create tasty fish burgers and make superb vegetarian versions from ingredients as different as beans and sweet potatoes. 'Extras' now extend far beyond merely adding a slice of cheese – although a genuine home-made cheeseburger is a barbecue delight – and recipes include marinades, spices, herbs, vegetables, nuts and fruit. There's sure to be the perfect burger for everyone, whether meaty and full of fiery Cajun flavours or a light-textured, moist mixture of apples and cheese – even for people who profess to dislike them.

the classic hamburger

ingredients

SERVES 4–6

450 g/1 lb rump steak or
   topside, freshly minced

1 onion, grated

2–4 garlic cloves, crushed

2 tsp wholegrain mustard

2 tbsp olive oil

450 g/1 lb onions, finely
   sliced

2 tsp light muscovado sugar

pepper

hamburger buns, to serve

method

1 Place the minced steak, onion, garlic, mustard and pepper in a large bowl and mix together. Shape into 4–6 equal-sized burgers, then cover and leave to chill for 30 minutes.

2 Meanwhile, heat the oil in a heavy-based frying pan. Add the onions and sauté over a low heat for 10–15 minutes, or until the onions have caramelized. Add the sugar after 8 minutes and stir occasionally during cooking. Drain well on kitchen paper and keep warm.

3 Preheat the barbecue. Cook the burgers over hot coals for 3–5 minutes on each side or until cooked to personal preference. Serve in hamburger buns with the onions.

cheese & bacon burgers

ingredients

SERVES 4

450 g/1 lb best steak mince

4 onions

2–4 garlic cloves, crushed

2–3 tsp grated fresh
    horseradish or 1–1$^{1}/_{2}$ tbsp
    creamed horseradish

8 lean back bacon rashers

2 tbsp sunflower oil

4 cheese slices

pepper

hamburger buns, to serve

method

1 Place the steak mince in a large bowl. Finely grate 1 of the onions and add to the steak mince in the bowl.

2 Add the garlic, horseradish and pepper to the steak mixture in the bowl. Mix together, then shape into 4 equal-sized burgers. Wrap each burger in 2 rashers of bacon, then cover and leave to chill for 30 minutes.

3 Preheat the barbecue. Slice the remaining onions. Heat the oil in a frying pan. Add the onions and cook over a medium heat for 8–10 minutes, stirring frequently, until the onions are golden brown. Drain on kitchen paper and keep warm.

4 Cook the burgers over hot coals for 3–5 minutes on each side, or until cooked through. Top each burger with a slice of cheese for the last minute of cooking. Serve in hamburger buns.

hamburgers with chilli & basil

ingredients

SERVES 4

650 g/1 lb 7 oz minced beef

1 red pepper, deseeded and
    finely chopped

1 garlic clove, finely chopped

2 small red chillies, deseeded
    and finely chopped

1 tbsp chopped fresh basil

$1/2$ tsp ground cumin

salt and pepper

sprigs of fresh basil,
    to garnish

hamburger buns, to serve

method

1 Put the minced beef, red pepper, garlic, chillies, chopped basil and cumin into a bowl and mix until well combined. Season with salt and pepper. Using your hands, form the mixture into burger shapes.

2 Preheat the barbecue. Cook the burgers over hot coals for 5–8 minutes on each side, or until cooked through. Garnish with sprigs of basil and serve in hamburger buns.

blt burger with asparagus

ingredients

SERVES 4–6

225 g/8 oz back bacon
    rashers
450 g/1 lb best steak mince
1 onion, grated
2–4 garlic cloves, crushed
1–2 tbsp sunflower oil
salt and pepper

dip

175 g/6 oz baby asparagus
    spears
1 tbsp lemon juice
1 small ripe avocado, peeled,
    stoned and finely chopped
2 firm tomatoes, peeled,
    deseeded and finely
    chopped
150 ml/5 fl oz crème fraîche
salt and pepper

to serve

hamburger buns
lettuce leaves
tomato slices

method

1 Remove any rind and fat from the bacon rashers and chop finely.

2 Place the bacon, steak mince, onion, garlic and salt and pepper in a large bowl and mix well. Shape into 4–6 equal-sized burgers, then cover and leave to chill for 30 minutes.

3 To make the dip, trim the asparagus and cook in a saucepan of lightly salted boiling water for 5 minutes, then drain and plunge into cold water. When cold, drain and finely chop half the spears into a bowl and reserve the rest to serve. Sprinkle the lemon juice over the avocado. Stir in the avocado, tomatoes and crème fraîche. Add salt and pepper to taste, cover and leave to chill until required.

4 Preheat the barbecue. Lightly brush the burgers with the oil, and cook over hot coals for 3–4 minutes on each side, or until cooked to personal preference. Serve the burgers in hamburger buns with lettuce, topped with a tomato slice, asparagus spear, and a dollop of the dip.

minty lamb burgers

ingredients

SERVES 4–6

1 red pepper, deseeded and
     cut into quarters
1 yellow pepper, deseeded
     and cut into quarters
1 red onion, cut into thick
     wedges
1 baby aubergine (115 g/4 oz),
     cut into wedges
2 tbsp olive oil
450 g/1 lb fresh lamb mince
2 tbsp freshly grated
     Parmesan cheese
1 tbsp chopped fresh mint
salt and pepper

minty mustard
mayonnaise
4 tbsp mayonnaise
1 tsp Dijon mustard
1 tbsp chopped fresh mint

to serve
hamburger buns
shredded lettuce
grilled vegetables, such as
     peppers and cherry
     tomatoes

method

1 Preheat the grill to medium. Place the peppers, onion and aubergine on a foil-lined grill rack, brush the aubergine with 1 tablespoon of the oil and cook under the hot grill for 10–12 minutes, or until charred. Remove from the grill, leave to cool, then peel the peppers. Place all the vegetables in a food processor and, using the pulse button, chop.

2 Add the lamb mince, Parmesan cheese, chopped mint and salt and pepper to the food processor and blend until the mixture comes together. Scrape on to a board and shape into 4–6 equal-sized burgers. Cover and leave to chill for at least 30 minutes.

3 To make the minty mustard mayonnaise, blend the mayonnaise with the mustard and chopped fresh mint. Cover and chill until required.

4 Preheat the barbecue. Lightly brush the burgers with the remaining oil, and cook over hot coals for 3–4 minutes on each side, or until cooked to personal preference. Serve the burgers in hamburger buns with the shredded lettuce and prepared mayonnaise, and a selection of grilled vegetables on the side.

lamb & feta cheese burgers

ingredients

SERVES 4–6

450 g/1 lb fresh lamb mince

225 g/8 oz feta cheese, crumbled

2 garlic cloves, crushed

6 spring onions, finely chopped

85 g/3 oz prunes, chopped

25 g/1 oz pine kernels, toasted

55 g/2 oz fresh wholemeal breadcrumbs

1 tbsp chopped fresh rosemary

1 tbsp sunflower oil

salt and pepper

method

1 Place the lamb mince in a large bowl with the feta, garlic, spring onions, prunes, pine kernels and breadcrumbs. Mix well, breaking up any lumps of mince.

2 Add the rosemary and salt and pepper to the lamb mixture in the bowl. Mix together, then shape into 4–6 equal-sized burgers. Cover and leave to chill for 30 minutes.

3 Preheat the barbecue. Brush the burgers lightly with oil and cook over hot coals for 4 minutes before turning over and brushing with the remaining oil. Continue to cook for 4 minutes, or until cooked to personal preference. Serve.

pork burgers with tangy orange marinade

ingredients

SERVES 4–6

450 g/1 lb pork fillet, cut into
    small pieces

3 tbsp Seville orange
    marmalade

2 tbsp orange juice

1 tbsp balsamic vinegar

225 g/8 oz parsnips,
    cut into chunks

1 tbsp finely grated orange rind

2 garlic cloves, crushed

6 spring onions, finely
    chopped

1 courgette (175 g/6 oz),
    grated

1 tbsp sunflower oil

salt and pepper

lettuce leaves, to serve

hamburger buns, to serve

method

1 Place the pork in a shallow dish. Place the marmalade, orange juice and vinegar in a small saucepan and heat, stirring, until the marmalade has melted. Pour the marinade over the pork. Cover and leave for at least 30 minutes, or longer if time permits. Remove the pork, reserving the marinade. Mince the pork into a large bowl.

2 Meanwhile, cook the parsnips in a saucepan of boiling water for 15–20 minutes, or until cooked. Drain, then mash and add to the pork. Stir in the orange rind, garlic, spring onions, courgette and salt and pepper to taste. Mix together, then shape into 4–6 equal-sized burgers. Cover and leave to chill for at least 30 minutes.

3 Preheat the barbecue. Lightly brush each burger with a little oil and then add them to the barbecue grill, cooking over medium–hot coals for 4–6 minutes on each side, or until thoroughly cooked. Boil the reserved marinade for at least 5 minutes, then pour into a small jug or bowl. Serve with the lettuce leaves in hamburger buns.

barbecued cajun pork burgers

ingredients

SERVES 4–6

225 g/8 oz sweet potatoes,
    cut into chunks

450 g/1 lb fresh pork mince

1 Granny Smith or other
    eating apple, peeled,
    cored and grated

2 tsp Cajun seasoning

2 onions

1 tbsp chopped fresh
    coriander

2 tbsp sunflower oil

8–12 lean back bacon
    rashers

salt and pepper

method

1 Cook the sweet potato in a saucepan of lightly salted boiling water for 15–20 minutes, or until soft when pierced with a fork. Drain well, then mash and reserve.

2 Place the pork mince in a bowl, add the mashed potato, grated apple and Cajun seasoning. Grate 1 of the onions and add to the mince mixture with salt and pepper to taste and the chopped coriander. Mix together, then shape into 4–6 equal-sized burgers. Cover and leave to chill for 1 hour.

3 Preheat the barbecue. Slice the remaining onion. Heat 1 tablespoon of the oil in a frying pan. Add the onion and cook over a low heat for 10–12 minutes, stirring until soft. Remove the frying pan from the heat and reserve. Wrap each burger in 2 rashers of bacon.

4 Cook the burgers over hot coals, brushing with the remaining oil for 4–5 minutes on each side, or until thoroughly cooked. Serve with the fried onions.

the ultimate chicken burger

ingredients

SERVES 4

4 large chicken breast fillets,
    skinned
1 large egg white
1 tbsp cornflour
1 tbsp plain flour
1 egg, beaten
55 g/2 oz fresh white
    breadcrumbs
2 tbsp sunflower oil
2 beef tomatoes, sliced

to serve

hamburger buns
shredded lettuce
mayonnaise

method

1 Place the chicken breasts between 2 sheets of baking paper and flatten slightly using a meat mallet or a rolling pin. Beat the egg white and cornflour together, then brush over the chicken. Cover and leave to chill for 30 minutes, then coat in the plain flour.

2 Place the egg yolk and breadcrumbs in 2 separate bowls and coat the burgers first in the egg, allowing any excess to drip back into the bowl, then in the breadcrumbs.

3 Preheat the barbecue. Lightly brush each burger with a little oil and then add them to the barbecue grill, cooking over medium–hot coals for 6–8 minutes on each side, or until thoroughly cooked. If you are in doubt, it is worth cutting one of the burgers in half. If there is any sign of pinkness, cook for a little longer to get that nice barbecue taste. Add the tomato slices to the grill rack for the last 1–2 minutes of the cooking time to heat through. Serve the burgers in hamburger buns with the shredded lettuce, cooked tomato slices and mayonnaise.

bacon-wrapped chicken burgers

ingredients

SERVES 4

450 g/1 lb fresh chicken mince

1 onion, grated

2 garlic cloves, crushed

55 g/2 oz pine kernels, toasted

55 g/2 oz Gruyère cheese, grated

2 tbsp fresh snipped chives

2 tbsp wholemeal flour

8 lean back bacon rashers

1–2 tbsp sunflower oil

salt and pepper

to serve

hamburger buns

shredded lettuce

red onion slices

method

1 Place the chicken mince, onion, garlic, pine kernels, cheese, chives and salt and pepper to taste in a food processor. Using the pulse button, blend the mixture together using short, sharp bursts. Scrape out on to a board and shape into 4 equal-sized burgers. Coat in the flour, then cover and leave to chill for 1 hour.

2 Wrap each burger with 2 bacon rashers, securing in place with a wooden cocktail stick.

3 Preheat the barbecue. When hot, lightly brush the burgers with oil and cook over medium–hot coals for 5–6 minutes on each side, or until cooked through. Remove the cocktail sticks and serve in hamburger buns with shredded lettuce and sliced red onion.

turkey & tarragon burgers

ingredients

SERVES 4

55 g/2 oz bulgar wheat
450 g/1 lb fresh turkey mince
1 tbsp finely grated orange
      rind
1 red onion, finely chopped
1 yellow pepper, deseeded,
      peeled and finely chopped
25 g/1 oz toasted flaked
      almonds
1 tbsp chopped fresh tarragon
1–2 tbsp sunflower oil
salt and pepper

to serve
hamburger buns
tomato relish
lettuce leaves
tomato slices
onion slices

method

1 Cook the bulgar wheat in a saucepan of lightly salted boiling water for 10–15 minutes, or according to the packet instructions.

2 Drain the bulgar wheat and place in a bowl with the turkey mince, orange rind, onion, yellow pepper, almonds, tarragon and salt and pepper. Mix together, then shape into 4 equal-sized burgers. Cover and leave to chill for 1 hour.

3 Preheat the barbecue. When hot, lightly brush the burgers with oil and cook over hot coals for 5–6 minutes on each side, or until cooked through. Serve in hamburger buns with tomato relish and lettuce leaves, with sliced tomato and onion on the side.

mexican turkey burgers

ingredients

SERVES 4

450 g/1 lb fresh turkey mince

200 g/7 oz canned refried
   beans

2–4 garlic cloves, crushed

1–2 fresh jalapeño chillies,
   deseeded and finely
   chopped

2 tbsp tomato purée

1 tbsp chopped fresh
   coriander

1 tbsp sunflower oil

salt and pepper

to serve

hamburger buns

shredded lettuce

salsa

guacamole

tortilla chips

method

1 Place the turkey mince in a bowl and break up any large lumps. Beat the refried beans until smooth, then add to the turkey in the bowl.

2 Add the garlic, chillies, tomato purée, coriander, salt and pepper and mix together. Shape into 4 equal-sized burgers, then cover and leave to chill for 1 hour.

3 Preheat the barbecue. When hot, lightly brush the burgers with oil and cook over hot coals for 5–6 minutes on each side, or until cooked through. Serve the Mexican turkey burgers in hamburger buns with shredded lettuce, salsa and guacamole, with tortilla chips on the side.

duck burgers with sweet apple & plum relish

ingredients

SERVES 4

2 apples

450 g/1 lb fresh duck breast meat, fat removed and minced

3 tbsp prepared plum sauce

6 spring onions, finely chopped

2 garlic cloves, crushed

1–1 1/2 tsp dried crushed chillies

55 g/2 oz dried cranberries

1 tbsp sunflower oil

1 tbsp butter

2–3 tsp demerara sugar

sweet apple and plum relish

150 ml/5 fl oz prepared apple sauce

salt and pepper

method

1 Peel, core and grate 1 of the apples and place in a large bowl with the minced duck, 1 tablespoon of the plum sauce, spring onions, garlic, 1/2–1 teaspoon of chillies, half the cranberries and salt and pepper to taste. Mix together, then shape into 4 equal-sized burgers. Cover and leave to chill for 1 hour.

2 Preheat the barbecue. When hot, lightly brush the burgers with oil and cook over hot coals for 3–4 minutes on each side, or until cooked to personal preference. Keep warm.

3 Peel, core and slice the remaining apple. Melt the butter in a frying pan. Add the apple, sprinkle with the sugar and cook for 3–4 minutes, or until slightly softened and lightly caramelized. Remove the frying pan from the heat.

4 To make the relish, heat the apple sauce, remaining chillies, cranberries and plum sauce for 3 minutes, stirring occasionally season with salt and pepper to taste. Keep warm until ready to serve with the burgers.

fish burgers

ingredients

SERVES 4

140 g/5 oz potatoes, cut into
    chunks
225 g/8 oz cod fillet, skinned
225 g/8 oz smoked haddock,
    skinned
1 tbsp grated lemon rind
1 tbsp chopped fresh parsley
1–2 tbsp plain flour
1 egg, beaten
85 g/3 oz fresh white
    breadcrumbs
2 tbsp sunflower oil
salt and pepper
hamburger buns, to serve

method

1 Cook the potatoes in a saucepan of lightly
salted boiling water for 15–20 minutes, or until
tender. Drain well and mash. Chop the fish
into small pieces, then place in a food
processor with the mashed potatoes, lemon
rind, parsley and salt and pepper to taste.
Using the pulse button, blend together. Shape
into 4 equal-sized burgers and coat in flour.
Cover and leave to chill for 30 minutes.

2 Place the egg and breadcrumbs in
2 separate bowls and coat the burgers first
in the egg, allowing any excess to drip back
into the bowl, then in the breadcrumbs.
Leave to chill for a further 30 minutes.

3 Preheat the barbecue. Brush the burgers
lightly with oil and cook over hot coals for
4–5 minutes on each side, or until golden
and cooked through. Serve in toasted
hamburger buns.

salmon burgers with spinach & pine kernels

ingredients

SERVES 4–6

300 g/10¹/₂ oz potatoes,
    cut into chunks

450 g/1 lb fresh salmon fillet,
    skinned

175 g/6 oz fresh spinach
    leaves

55 g/2 oz pine kernels,
    toasted

2 tbsp finely grated lemon rind

1 tbsp chopped fresh parsley

2 tbsp wholemeal flour

200 ml/7 fl oz crème fraîche

4-cm/1¹/₂-inch piece
    cucumber, peeled and
    finely chopped

2 tbsp sunflower oil

salt and pepper

to serve
hamburger buns
cherry tomatoes

method

1 Cook the potatoes in a saucepan of lightly salted boiling water for 15–20 minutes, or until tender. Drain well, then mash and reserve. Chop the salmon into chunks.

2 Reserve a few spinach leaves for serving, then blanch the remainder in a saucepan of boiling water for 2 minutes. Drain, squeezing out any excess moisture, then chop.

3 Place the spinach in a food processor with the salmon, potatoes, pine kernels, 1 tablespoon of the lemon rind, parsley and salt and pepper and, using the pulse button, blend together. Shape into 4-6 equal-sized burger, coat in the flour, then cover and leave to chill for 1 hour.

4 Mix the crème fraîche, remaining lemon rind and cucumber together in a bowl, then cover and leave to chill until required.

5 Preheat the barbecue. When hot, lightly brush the burgers with oil and cook over hot coals for 4–6 minutes on each side, or until cooked through. Serve the burgers in hamburger buns with the reserved spinach leaves, crème fraiche and cucumber dip and cherry tomatoes on the side.

fresh tuna burgers with mango salsa

ingredients

SERVES 4–6

225 g/8 oz sweet potatoes, chopped

450 g/1 lb fresh tuna steaks

6 spring onions, finely chopped

175 g/6 oz courgette, grated

1 fresh red jalapeño chilli, deseeded and finely chopped

2 tbsp prepared mango chutney

1 tbsp sunflower oil

salt

lettuce leaves, to serve

mango salsa

1 large ripe mango, peeled and stoned

2 ripe tomatoes, finely chopped

1 fresh red jalapeño chilli, deseeded and finely chopped

4-cm/1^1/$_2$-inch piece cucumber, finely diced

1 tbsp chopped fresh coriander

1–2 tsp clear honey

method

1 Cook the sweet potatoes in a saucepan of lightly salted boiling water for 15–20 minutes, or until tender. Drain well, then mash and place in a food processor. Cut the tuna into chunks and add to the potatoes.

2 Add the spring onions, courgette, chilli and mango chutney to the food processor and, using the pulse button, blend together. Shape into 4–6 equal-sized burgers, then cover and leave to chill for 1 hour.

3 Meanwhile make the salsa. Slice the mango flesh, reserving 8–12 good slices for serving. Finely chop the remainder of the mango, then mix with the tomatoes, chilli, cucumber, coriander and honey. Mix well, then spoon into a small bowl. Cover and leave for 30 minutes to allow the flavours to develop.

4 Preheat the barbecue. Brush the burgers lightly with oil and cook over hot coals for 4–6 minutes on each side, or until piping hot. Serve with the mango salsa, garnished with lettuce leaves and the reserved slices of mango.

the ultimate vegetarian burger

ingredients

SERVES 4–6

85 g/3 oz brown rice

400 g/14 oz canned flageolet beans, drained

115 g/4 oz unsalted cashew nuts

3 garlic cloves

1 red onion, cut into wedges

115 g/4 oz sweetcorn kernels

2 tbsp tomato purée

1 tbsp chopped fresh oregano

2 tbsp wholemeal flour

2 tbsp sunflower oil

salt and pepper

to serve

hamburger buns

lettuce leaves

tomato slices

cheese slices

method

1 Cook the rice in a saucepan of lightly salted boiling water for 20 minutes, or following the packet instructions, until tender. Drain and place in a food processor.

2 Add the beans, cashew nuts, garlic, onion, sweetcorn, tomato purée, oregano and salt and pepper to the rice in the food processor and, using the pulse button, blend together. Shape into 4–6 equal-sized burgers, then coat in the flour. Cover and leave to chill for 1 hour.

3 Preheat the barbecue. Brush the burgers with oil. When the barbecue is hot, cook the burgers over medium–hot coals for 5–6 minutes on each side, or until cooked and piping hot. Serve the burgers in hamburger buns with the salad leaves, and tomato and cheese slices.

three-bean burgers with green mayo

ingredients

SERVES 4–6

300 g/10¹/₂ oz canned
cannellini beans, drained

300 g/10¹/₂ oz canned black-
eyed beans, drained

300 g/10¹/₂ oz canned red
kidney beans, drained
and rinsed

1 fresh red chilli, deseeded

4 shallots, cut into quarters

2 celery sticks, roughly
chopped

55 g/2 oz fresh wholemeal
breadcrumbs

1 tbsp chopped fresh
coriander

2 tbsp wholemeal flour

2 tbsp sunflower oil

salt and pepper

hamburger buns, to serve

green mayo

6 tbsp prepared mayonnaise

2 tbsp chopped fresh parsley
or mint

1 tbsp chopped cucumber

3 spring onions, finely
chopped

method

1 Place the beans, chilli, shallots, celery,
breadcrumbs, coriander and salt and pepper
in a food processor and, using the pulse button,
blend together. Shape into 4–6 equal-sized
burgers, coat in the flour, then cover and leave
to chill for 1 hour

2 To make the green mayo, place the
mayonnaise, parsley, cucumber and spring
onions in a bowl and mix together. Cover
and chill until required.

3 Preheat the barbecue. Brush the burgers
lightly with oil and cook over hot coals for
5–6 minutes on each side, or until piping
hot. Serve in hamburger buns with the
green mayo.

sweet potato & halloumi burgers

ingredients

SERVES 4–6

450 g/1 lb sweet potatoes, peeled and cut into chunks

175 g/6 oz broccoli florets

2–3 garlic cloves, crushed

1 red onion, finely chopped or grated

$1^1/_2$–2 fresh red jalapeño chillies, deseeded and finely chopped

175 g/6 oz halloumi cheese, grated

2 tbsp wholemeal flour

2–3 tbsp sunflower oil

450 g/1 lb onions, sliced

1 tbsp chopped fresh coriander

salt and pepper

hamburger buns, to serve

salad greens, to serve

method

1 Cook the sweet potato in a saucepan of lightly salted boiling water for 15–20 minutes, or until tender. Drain and mash. Cut the broccoli into small pieces, cook in a separate saucepan of boiling water for 3 minutes, then drain and plunge into cold water. Drain again, then add to the mashed sweet potato.

2 Stir in the garlic, onion, chilli, grated cheese and salt and pepper. Mix well and shape into 4–6 equal-sized burgers, then coat in the flour. Cover and leave to chill for at least 1 hour.

3 Heat $1^1/_2$ tablespoons of the oil in a heavy-based frying pan. Add the onions and fry over medium heat for 12–15 minutes, or until softened. Stir in the coriander and reserve.

4 Preheat the barbecue. When hot, lightly brush the burgers with the remaining oil and cook over hot coals for 5–6 minutes on each side, or until piping hot. Serve the burgers and onions in hamburger buns with salad greens.

vegetarian chilli burgers

ingredients

SERVES 4–6

85 g/3 oz bulgar wheat

300 g/10^1/$_2$ oz canned red
    kidney beans, drained
    and rinsed

300 g/10^1/$_2$ oz canned
    cannellini beans, drained

1–2 fresh red jalapeño
    chillies, deseeded and
    roughly chopped

2–3 garlic cloves

6 spring onions, roughly
    chopped

1 yellow pepper, deseeded,
    peeled and chopped

1 tbsp chopped fresh
    coriander

115 g/4 oz mature Cheddar
    cheese, grated

2 tbsp wholemeal flour

1–2 tbsp sunflower oil

1 large tomato, sliced

salt and pepper

hamburger buns, to serve

method

1 Cook the bulgar wheat in a saucepan of lightly salted water for 12 minutes, or until cooked. Drain and reserve.

2 Place the beans in a food processor with the chillies, garlic, spring onions, pepper, coriander and half the cheese. Using the pulse button, chop finely. Add to the cooked bulgar wheat with salt and pepper to taste. Mix well, then shape into 4–6 equal-sized burgers. Coat the burgers in the flour and cover and leave to chill for 1 hour.

3 Preheat the barbecue. When hot, lightly brush the burgers with oil and cook over hot coals for 4–6 minutes on each side, or until cooked to personal preference. Place 1–2 slices of tomato on top of each burger and sprinkle with the remaining cheese. Cook for a further 2–3 minutes, or until the cheese starts to melt. Serve the burgers in hamburger buns.

mushroom burgers

ingredients

SERVES 4

115 g/4 oz mushrooms

1 carrot

1 onion

1 courgette

2 tsp sunflower oil, plus extra
     for brushing

25 g/1 oz peanuts

115 g/4 oz fresh white
     breadcrumbs

1 tbsp chopped fresh parsley

1 tsp yeast extract

1 tbsp plain flour, for dusting

salt and pepper

method

1 Using a sharp knife, finely chop the mushrooms, then chop the carrot, onion and courgette and reserve. Heat the oil in a heavy-based frying pan, add the mushrooms and cook, stirring, for 8 minutes, or until all the moisture has evaporated. Using a slotted spoon, transfer the cooked mushrooms to a large bowl.

2 Put the carrot, onion, courgette and peanuts into a food processor and process until finely chopped. Transfer to the bowl containing the mushrooms and stir in the breadcrumbs, chopped parsley and yeast extract. Season to taste with salt and pepper. Lightly flour your hands and form the mixture into 4 burgers. Place on a large plate, cover with clingfilm and leave to chill in the refrigerator for at least 1 hour and up to 1 day.

3 Preheat the barbecue. Brush the mushroom burgers with the sunflower oil and cook over hot coals for 8–10 minutes. Serve.

blue cheese & apple burgers

ingredients

SERVES 4–6

175 g/6 oz new potatoes

225 g/8 oz mixed nuts, such
as pecans, almonds and
hazelnuts

1 onion, roughly chopped

225 g/8 oz apples

175 g/6 oz blue cheese,
crumbled

55 g/2 oz fresh wholemeal
breadcrumbs

2 tbsp wholemeal flour

1–2 tbsp sunflower oil

salt and pepper

to serve

hamburger buns

salad greens

red onion slices

method

1 Cook the potatoes in a saucepan of boiling water for 15–20 minutes, or until tender when pierced with a fork. Drain and, using a potato masher, crush into small pieces. Place in a large bowl.

2 Place the nuts and onion in a food processor and, using the pulse button, chop finely. Add the nuts, onion, apple, cheese and breadcrumbs to the potatoes in the bowl. Season with salt and pepper to taste. Mix well, then shape into 4–6 equal-sized burgers. Coat in the flour, then cover and leave to chill for 1 hour.

3 Preheat the barbecue. When hot, lightly brush the burgers with the oil and cook over hot coals for 5–6 minutes on each side, or until cooked through. Serve the burgers in hamburger buns with salad greens and red onion slices.

butternut squash & polenta burgers

ingredients

SERVES 4–6

450 g/1 lb butternut squash
  (225 g/8 oz after peeling
  and deseeding), cut into
  chunks
150 ml/5 fl oz water
85 g/3 oz instant polenta
115 g/4 oz celeriac, peeled
  and grated
6 spring onions, finely
  chopped
115 g/4 oz pecan nuts,
  chopped
55 g/2 oz freshly grated
  Parmesan cheese
2 tbsp chopped fresh mixed
  herbs
2 tbsp wholemeal flour
2 tbsp sunflower oil
salt and pepper

to serve
hamburger buns
salad greens
tomato slices
chips

method

1 Cook the butternut squash in a saucepan of boiling water for 15–20 minutes, or until tender. Drain and finely chop or mash. Place the water in a separate saucepan and bring to the boil. Slowly pour in the polenta in a steady stream and cook over a gentle heat, stirring, for 5 minutes, or until thick.

2 Remove the saucepan from the heat and stir in the butternut squash, celeriac, spring onions, pecan nuts, cheese, herbs and salt and pepper to taste. Mix well, then shape into 4–6 equal-sized burgers. Coat the burgers in the flour and cover and leave to chill for 1 hour.

3 Preheat the barbecue. When hot, lightly brush the burgers with oil and cook over hot coals for 5–6 minutes on each side, or until cooked through. Serve the burgers in hamburger buns with salad greens and tomato slices, and chips on the side.

vegetable & tofu burgers

ingredients

SERVES 4–6

115 g/4 oz rice

115 g/4 oz carrot, grated

6 spring onions, roughly
    chopped

55 g/2 oz unsalted peanuts

85 g/3 oz fresh beansprouts

225 g/8 oz firm tofu (drained
    weight), finely chopped

1 tsp prepared ginger pulp

$^{1}/_{2}$–1 tsp crushed chillies

1–2 tbsp sunflower oil

to serve

hamburger buns

salad greens

relish

method

1 Cook the rice in a saucepan of lightly boiling water for 12–15 minutes, or until soft. Drain and place in a large bowl.

2 Place the carrot, spring onions and peanuts in a food processor and, using the pulse button, chop finely. Add the rice, beansprouts, tofu, ginger and chillies and blend together. Shape into 4–6 equal-sized burgers, firmly pressing them together. Cover and leave to chill for 1 hour.

3 Preheat the barbecue. When hot, lightly brush the burgers with oil and cook over hot coals for 5–6 minutes on each side, or until cooked through. Serve the burgers in hamburger buns with salad greens and relish.

family favourites

The sun's shining, the cover's off the barbecue and now you must make the decision of what to cook. Everyone has their own special favourite but there are some recipes that are always popular with all the family. Meat is many people's first choice, whether sizzling steaks, spicy ribs, succulent chops or scrumptious sausages. Kids, in particular, love chicken, especially if they can eat it with their fingers – the stickier they get, the more fun they have. Even adults enjoy nibbling on spicy wings or marinated drumsticks.

Fish-lovers will stake a claim for salmon and tuna, both of them ideal for barbecue grilling and absolutely delicious served with a fresh salsa. Less robust fish is great cooked in parcels and there's something specially appetizing about unwrapping it on your plate to release the aromas and reveal the finished dish.

Vegetarian sausages are perennially popular with those who don't eat meat and when they are home-made, they are a real treat. On the other hand, cheese, vegetables and a barbecue go together so naturally that even meat eaters will want to share these vegetarian delights.

There's only one problem with this abundance of family favourites – you are so spoiled for choice, how can you decide which to cook first?

barbecued steak fajitas

ingredients

SERVES 4

2 tbsp sunflower oil, plus
    extra for oiling

finely grated rind of 1 lime

1 tbsp lime juice

2 garlic cloves, crushed

1/4 tsp ground coriander

1/4 tsp ground cumin

pinch of sugar

1 piece of rump steak, about
    675 g/1 lb 8 oz and
    2 cm/3/4 inch thick

4 wheat tortillas

1 avocado

2 tomatoes, thinly sliced

4 tbsp soured cream

4 spring onions, thinly sliced

salt and pepper

method

1 To make the marinade, put the oil, lime rind and juice, garlic, coriander, cumin, sugar and salt and pepper to taste into a shallow, non-metallic dish large enough to hold the steak and mix together. Add the steak and turn in the marinade to coat it. Cover and leave to marinate in the refrigerator for 6–8 hours or up to 24 hours, turning occasionally.

2 When ready to cook, preheat the barbecue. Using a slotted spoon, remove the steak from the marinade, put on to an oiled grill rack and cook over a medium heat for 5 minutes for rare or 8–10 minutes for medium, turning the steak frequently and basting once or twice with any remaining marinade.

3 Meanwhile, warm the tortillas according to the instructions on the packet. Peel and slice the avocado.

4 Thinly slice the steak across the grain and arrange an equal quantity of the slices on one side of each tortilla. Add the tomato and avocado slices, top with a spoonful of soured cream and sprinkle over the spring onions. Fold over and eat immediately.

boozy beef steaks

ingredients

SERVES 4

4 beef steaks

4 tbsp whisky or brandy

2 tbsp soy sauce

1 tbsp dark muscovado sugar

tomato slices

pepper

fresh parsley sprigs,
    to garnish

garlic bread, to serve

method

1 Make a few cuts in the edge of the fat on each steak. This will stop the meat from curling as it cooks. Place the meat in a shallow, non-metallic dish.

2 Mix the whisky, soy sauce, sugar and pepper to taste together in a small bowl, stirring until the sugar dissolves. Pour the mixture over the steak. Cover with clingfilm and leave to marinate in the refrigerator for at least 2 hours.

3 Preheat the barbecue. Cook the meat over hot coals, searing the meat over the hottest part of the barbecue for 2 minutes on each side.

4 Move the meat to an area with slightly less intense heat and cook for a further 4–10 minutes on each side, depending on how well done you like your steaks. To test if the meat is cooked, insert the point of a sharp knife into the meat – the juices will run from red when the meat is still rare, to clear as it becomes well cooked.

5 Lightly barbecue the tomato slices for 1–2 minutes. Transfer the meat and the tomatoes to warmed serving plates. Garnish with fresh parsley sprigs and serve with garlic bread.

meatballs on sticks

ingredients

SERVES 8

4 pork and herb sausages

115 g/4 oz fresh beef mince

85 g/3 oz fresh white
    breadcrumbs

1 onion, finely chopped

2 tbsp chopped mixed fresh
    herbs, such as parsley,
    thyme and sage

1 egg

salt and pepper

sunflower oil, for brushing

method

1 Preheat the barbecue. Remove the sausage
meat from the skins, place in a large bowl and
break up with a fork. Add the beef mince,
breadcrumbs, onion, herbs and egg. Season
to taste with salt and pepper and stir well with
a wooden spoon until thoroughly mixed.

2 Form the mixture into small balls, about the
size of a golf ball, between the palms of your
hands. Spear each one with a cocktail stick
and brush with oil.

3 Cook over medium–hot coals, turning
frequently and brushing with more oil as
necessary, for 10 minutes, or until cooked
through. Transfer to a large serving plate and
serve immediately.

barbecued pork sausages with thyme

ingredients

SERVES 4

1 garlic clove, finely chopped

1 onion, grated

1 small red chilli, deseeded
and finely chopped

450 g/1 lb lean minced pork

50 g/1¾ oz almonds, toasted
and ground

50 g/1¾ oz fresh
breadcrumbs

1 tbsp finely chopped fresh
thyme

salt and pepper

flour, for dusting

vegetable oil, for brushing

to serve

fresh finger rolls

slices of onion, lightly cooked

ketchup and/or mustard

method

1 Put the garlic, onion, chilli, pork, almonds, breadcrumbs and fresh thyme into a large bowl. Season well with salt and pepper and mix until well combined.

2 Using your hands, form the mixture into sausage shapes. Roll each sausage in a little flour, then transfer to a bowl, cover with clingfilm and refrigerate for 45 minutes.

3 Preheat the barbecue. Brush a piece of aluminium foil with oil, then put the sausages on the foil and brush them with a little more vegetable oil. Transfer the sausages and foil to the barbecue.

4 Barbecue over hot coals, turning the sausages frequently, for about 15 minutes, or until cooked right through. Serve with finger rolls, cooked sliced onion and tomato ketchup and/or mustard.

hot & spicy pork ribs

ingredients

SERVES 4

1 onion, chopped

2 garlic cloves, chopped

2.5-cm/1-inch piece fresh
   root ginger, sliced

1 fresh red chilli, deseeded
   and chopped

5 tbsp dark soy sauce

3 tbsp lime juice

1 tbsp palm or muscovado
   sugar

2 tbsp groundnut oil

1 kg/2 lb 4 oz pork spare ribs,
   separated

salt and pepper

few sprigs of flat-leaf parsley,
   to garnish

method

1 Preheat the barbecue. Put the onion, garlic, ginger, chilli and soy sauce into a food processor and process to a paste. Transfer to a jug and stir in the lime juice, sugar and oil and season to taste with salt and pepper.

2 The spare ribs must be pre-cooked before barbecuing, so place the spare ribs in a preheated wok or large, heavy-based saucepan and pour in the soy sauce mixture. Place on the hob and bring to the boil, then simmer over a low heat, stirring frequently, for 30 minutes. If the mixture appears to be drying out, add a little water.

3 Remove the spare ribs, reserving the sauce. Cook the ribs over medium–hot coals, turning and basting frequently with the sauce, for 20–30 minutes. Transfer to a large serving plate, garnish with a few sprigs of parsley, and serve immediately.

honey-glazed pork chops

ingredients

SERVES 4

4 lean pork loin chops

4 tbsp clear honey

1 tbsp dry sherry

4 tbsp orange juice

2 tbsp olive oil

2.5-cm/1-inch piece fresh
    ginger, grated

salt and pepper

sunflower oil, for oiling

method

1 Preheat the barbecue. Season the pork chops with salt and pepper to taste. Reserve while you make the glaze.

2 To make the glaze, place the honey, sherry, orange juice, olive oil and ginger in a small saucepan and heat gently, stirring constantly, until well blended.

3 Cook the pork chops on an oiled rack over hot coals for 5 minutes on each side.

4 Brush the chops with the glaze and barbecue for a further 2–4 minutes on each side, basting frequently with the glaze.

5 Transfer the pork chops to warmed serving plates and serve hot.

minty lamb chops

ingredients

SERVES 6

6 chump chops, about
175 g/6 oz each

150 ml/5 fl oz natural Greek
yogurt

2 garlic cloves, finely
chopped

1 tsp grated fresh ginger

1/4 tsp coriander seeds,
crushed

minty yogurt

1 tbsp olive oil, plus extra
for brushing

1 tbsp orange juice

1 tsp walnut oil

2 tbsp chopped fresh mint

salt and pepper

method

1 Place the chops in a large, shallow, non-metallic bowl. Mix half the yogurt, the garlic, ginger and coriander seeds together in a jug and season to taste with salt and pepper. Spoon the mixture over the chops, turning to coat, then cover with clingfilm and leave to marinate in the refrigerator for 2 hours, turning occasionally.

2 Preheat the barbecue. To make the minty yogurt, place the remaining yogurt, the olive oil, orange juice, walnut oil and mint in a small bowl and, using a hand-held blender, mix until thoroughly blended. Season to taste with salt and pepper. Cover the minted yogurt with clingfilm and leave to chill in the refrigerator until ready to serve.

3 Drain the chops, scraping off the marinade. Brush with olive oil and cook over medium–hot coals for 5–7 minutes on each side. Serve immediately with the minted yogurt.

spicy lamb steaks

ingredients

SERVES 4

4 lamb steaks, about
175 g/6 oz each
8 fresh rosemary sprigs
8 fresh bay leaves
2 tbsp olive oil

spicy marinade

2 tbsp sunflower oil
1 large onion, finely chopped
2 garlic cloves, finely
chopped
2 tbsp jerk seasoning
1 tbsp curry paste
1 tsp grated fresh root ginger
400 g/14 oz canned chopped
tomatoes
4 tbsp Worcestershire sauce
3 tbsp light muscovado sugar
salt and pepper

method

1 To make the marinade, heat the oil in a
heavy-based saucepan. Add the onion and
garlic and cook, stirring occasionally, for
5 minutes, or until softened. Stir in the jerk
seasoning, curry paste and grated ginger and
cook, stirring constantly, for 2 minutes. Add
the tomatoes, Worcestershire sauce and sugar,
then season to taste with salt and pepper. Bring
to the boil, stirring constantly, then reduce
the heat and simmer for 15 minutes, or until
thickened. Remove from the heat and leave
to cool.

2 Place the lamb steaks between 2 sheets of
clingfilm and beat with the side of a rolling pin
to flatten. Transfer the steaks to a large, shallow,
non-metallic dish. Pour the marinade over
them, turning to coat. Cover with clingfilm
and leave to marinate in the refrigerator for
3 hours.

3 Preheat the barbecue. Drain the lamb,
reserving the marinade. Cook the lamb over
medium–hot coals, brushing frequently with
the marinade, for 5–7 minutes on each side.
Meanwhile, dip the rosemary and bay leaves
in the olive oil and cook on the barbecue for
3–5 minutes. Serve the lamb immediately with
the herbs.

spicy chicken wings

ingredients

SERVES 4

16 chicken wings

4 tbsp sunflower oil

4 tbsp light soy sauce

5-cm/2-inch piece fresh
	ginger, roughly chopped

2 garlic cloves, roughly
	chopped

juice and grated rind of
	1 lemon

2 tsp ground cinnamon

2 tsp ground turmeric

4 tbsp clear honey

salt and pepper

sauce

2 orange peppers

2 yellow peppers

sunflower oil, for brushing

125 ml/4 fl oz natural yogurt

2 tbsp dark soy sauce

2 tbsp chopped fresh
	coriander

method

1 Place the chicken wings in a large, shallow, non-metallic dish. Put the oil, soy sauce, ginger, garlic, lemon rind and juice, cinnamon, turmeric and honey into a food processor and process to a smooth purée. Season to taste with salt and pepper. Spoon the mixture over the chicken wings and turn until thoroughly coated, cover with clingfilm and leave to marinate in the refrigerator for up to 8 hours.

2 Preheat the barbecue. To make the sauce, brush the peppers with the oil and cook over hot coals, turning frequently, for 10 minutes, or until the skin is blackened and charred. Remove from the barbecue and leave to cool slightly, then peel off the skins and discard the seeds. Put the flesh into a food processor with the yogurt and process to a smooth purée. Transfer to a bowl and stir in the soy sauce and chopped coriander.

3 Drain the chicken wings, reserving the marinade. Cook over medium–hot coals, turning and brushing frequently with the reserved marinade, for 8–10 minutes, or until thoroughly cooked. Serve immediately with the sauce.

jerk chicken

ingredients

SERVES 4

4 lean chicken portions

1 bunch spring onions,
    trimmed

1–2 Scotch Bonnet chillies,
    deseeded

1 garlic clove

5-cm/2-inch piece ginger,
    peeled and roughly
    chopped

$1/2$ tsp dried thyme

$1/2$ tsp paprika

$1/4$ tsp ground allspice

pinch ground cinnamon

pinch ground cloves

4 tbsp white wine vinegar

3 tbsp light soy sauce

pepper

12 whole, barbecued chillies,
    to serve

method

1 Rinse the chicken portions and pat them dry on absorbent kitchen paper. Place them in a shallow dish.

2 Place the spring onions, chillies, garlic, ginger, thyme, paprika, allspice, cinnamon, cloves, wine vinegar, soy sauce and pepper to taste in a food processor and process until smooth.

3 Pour the spicy mixture over the chicken. Turn the chicken portions over so that they are well coated in the marinade.

4 Transfer the chicken portions to the refrigerator and leave to marinate for up to 24 hours.

5 Remove the chicken from the marinade and barbecue over medium–hot coals for about 30 minutes, turning the chicken over and basting occasionally with any remaining marinade, until the chicken is browned and cooked through.

6 Transfer the chicken portions to individual serving plates and serve with the barbecued, whole chillies.

cajun chicken

ingredients

SERVES 4

4 chicken drumsticks

4 chicken thighs

2 fresh corn cobs, husks and
   silks removed

85 g/3 oz butter, melted

few sprigs of flat-leaf parsley,
   to garnish

spice mix

2 tsp onion powder

2 tsp paprika

1^1/$_2$ tsp salt

1 tsp garlic powder

1 tsp dried thyme

1 tsp cayenne pepper

1 tsp ground black pepper

^{1}/$_2$ tsp ground white pepper

^{1}/$_4$ tsp ground cumin

method

1 Preheat the barbecue. Using a sharp knife, make 2–3 diagonal slashes in the chicken drumsticks and thighs, then place them in a large dish. Cut the corn cobs into thick slices and add them to the dish. Mix all the ingredients for the spice mix together in a small bowl.

2 Brush the chicken and corn with the melted butter and sprinkle with the spice mix. Toss to coat well.

3 Cook the chicken over medium–hot coals, turning occasionally, for 15 minutes, then add the corn slices and cook, turning occasionally, for a further 10–15 minutes, or until beginning to blacken slightly at the edges. Transfer to a large serving plate, garnish with some sprigs of parsley, and serve.

mustard & honey chicken drumsticks

ingredients

SERVES 4

8 chicken drumsticks

salad leaves, to serve

glaze

125 ml/4 fl oz clear honey

4 tbsp Dijon mustard

4 tbsp wholegrain mustard

4 tbsp white wine vinegar

2 tbsp sunflower oil

salt and pepper

method

1 Using a sharp knife, make 2–3 diagonal slashes in the chicken drumsticks and place them in a large, non-metallic dish.

2 Preheat the barbecue. Mix all the ingredients for the glaze together in a jug and season to taste with salt and pepper. Pour the glaze over the drumsticks, turning until the drumsticks are well coated. Cover with clingfilm and leave to marinate in the refrigerator for at least 1 hour.

3 Drain the chicken drumsticks, reserving the marinade. Cook the chicken over medium–hot coals, turning frequently and brushing with the reserved marinade, for 25–30 minutes, or until thoroughly cooked. Transfer to serving plates and serve immediately with the salad leaves.

spicy pitta pockets

ingredients

SERVES 4

500 g/1 lb 2 oz skinless,
    boneless chicken, cut into
    2.5-cm/1-inch cubes
3 tbsp natural yogurt
1 tsp chilli powder
3 tbsp lime juice
1 tbsp chopped fresh
    coriander
1 fresh green chilli, deseeded
    and finely chopped
1 tbsp sunflower oil
salt

chilli sauce

2 tbsp sunflower oil
1 onion, chopped
2 garlic cloves, crushed
4 large tomatoes, peeled,
    deseeded and chopped
2 fresh red chillies, deseeded
    and chopped
pinch of ground cumin
salt and pepper

to serve

4 pitta breads
1/4 iceberg lettuce, shredded
2 tomatoes, thinly sliced
8 spring onions, chopped
1 tbsp lemon juice
8 bottled jalapeño chillies,
    drained, to serve

method

1 Place the chicken in a large bowl. Mix the yogurt, chilli powder, lime juice, fresh coriander, green chilli and sunflower oil together in a jug and season to taste with salt. Pour the mixture over the chicken and turn until the chicken is coated. Cover with clingfilm and leave to marinate in the refrigerator for 2 hours.

2 Preheat the barbecue. To make the chilli sauce, heat the oil in a small saucepan. Add the onion and garlic and cook over a low heat, stirring occasionally, for 10 minutes, or until softened and golden. Add the tomatoes, chillies and cumin and season to taste with salt and pepper. Simmer gently for 15 minutes, or until reduced and thickened.

3 Set the saucepan of chilli sauce on the side of the barbecue to keep warm. Drain the chicken, reserving the marinade. Thread the chicken on to presoaked wooden skewers. Cook over medium–hot coals, turning and brushing frequently with the reserved marinade, for 6–10 minutes, or until thoroughly cooked. Meanwhile, slit the pitta breads with a sharp knife and toast briefly on the barbecue. To serve, remove the chicken from the skewers and fill the pitta breads with lettuce, tomato slices, spring onions and chicken. Sprinkle with lemon juice and top with the bottled chillies. Serve immediately with the chilli sauce.

charred fish

ingredients

SERVES 4

4 white fish steaks

1 tbsp paprika

1 tsp dried thyme

1 tsp cayenne pepper

1 tsp black pepper

1/2 tsp white pepper

1/2 tsp salt

1/4 tsp ground allspice

50 g/1 3/4 oz unsalted butter

3 tbsp sunflower oil

green beans, to serve

method

1 Preheat the barbecue. Rinse the fish steaks under cold running water and pat dry with kitchen paper.

2 Mix the paprika, thyme, cayenne, black and white peppers, salt and allspice together in a shallow dish.

3 Place the butter and sunflower oil in a small saucepan and heat gently, stirring occasionally, until the butter melts.

4 Brush the butter mixture liberally all over the fish steaks, on both sides, then dip the fish into the spicy mix until coated on both sides.

5 Cook the fish over hot coals for 3 minutes on each side, until cooked through. Continue to baste the fish with the remaining butter mixture during the cooking time. Serve with the green beans.

salmon with mango salsa

ingredients

SERVES 4

4 salmon steaks, about
175 g/6 oz each

finely grated rind and juice of
1 lime or 1/2 lemon

salt and pepper

salsa

1 large mango, peeled,
stoned and diced

1 red onion, finely chopped

2 passion fruit

2 fresh basil sprigs

2 tbsp lime juice

salt

method

1 Preheat the barbecue. Rinse the salmon steaks under cold running water, pat dry with kitchen paper and place in a large, shallow, non-metallic dish. Sprinkle with the lime rind and pour the juice over them. Season to taste with salt and pepper, cover and leave to stand while you make the salsa.

2 Place the mango flesh in a bowl with the onion. Cut the passion fruit in half and scoop out the seeds and pulp with a teaspoon into the bowl. Tear the basil leaves and add them to the bowl with the lime juice. Season to taste with salt and stir well. Cover with clingfilm and reserve until required.

3 Cook the salmon steaks over medium–hot coals for 3–4 minutes on each side. Serve immediately with the salsa.

chargrilled tuna with chilli salsa

ingredients

SERVES 4

4 tuna steaks, about 175 g/
    6 oz each
grated rind and juice of 1 lime
2 tbsp olive oil
salt and pepper
fresh coriander sprigs,
    to garnish
lettuce leaves, to garnish
crusty bread, to serve

chilli salsa
2 orange peppers
1 tbsp olive oil
juice of 1 lime
juice of 1 orange
2–3 fresh red chillies,
    deseeded and chopped
pinch of cayenne pepper

method

1 Rinse the tuna thoroughly under cold running water and pat dry with kitchen paper, then place in a large, shallow, non-metallic dish. Sprinkle with the lime rind and pour the juice and olive oil over the fish. Season to taste with salt and pepper, cover with clingfilm and leave to marinate in the refrigerator for up to 1 hour.

2 Preheat the barbecue. To make the salsa, brush the peppers with the olive oil and cook over hot coals, turning frequently, for 10 minutes, or until the skin is blackened and charred. Remove from the barbecue and leave to cool slightly, then peel off the skins and discard the seeds. Put the peppers into a food processor with the remaining salsa ingredients and process to a purée. Transfer to a bowl and season to taste with salt and pepper.

3 Cook the tuna over hot coals for 4–5 minutes on each side, until golden. Transfer to serving plates, garnish with coriander sprigs and lettuce leaves, and serve with the salsa and plenty of crusty bread.

cod & tomato parcels

ingredients

SERVES 4

4 cod steaks, about
175 g/6 oz each

2 tsp extra virgin olive oil

4 tomatoes, peeled and
chopped

25 g/1 oz fresh basil leaves,
torn into small pieces

4 tbsp white wine

salt and pepper

method

1 Preheat the barbecue. Rinse the cod steaks under cold running water and pat dry with kitchen paper. Using a sharp knife, cut out and discard the central bones. Cut out 4 rectangles, 33 x 20 cm/13 x 8 inches, from double-thickness foil and brush with the olive oil. Place a cod steak in the centre of each piece of foil.

2 Mix the tomatoes, basil and white wine together in a bowl and season to taste with salt and pepper. Spoon the tomato mixture equally on top of the fish. Bring up the sides of the foil and fold over securely.

3 Cook the cod parcels over hot coals for 3–5 minutes on each side. Transfer to 4 large serving plates and serve immediately in the parcels.

aubergine & mozzarella sandwich

ingredients

SERVES 2

1 large aubergine

1 tbsp lemon juice

3 tbsp olive oil

125 g/4^1/$_2$ oz grated
mozzarella cheese

2 sun-dried tomatoes,
chopped

salt and pepper

to serve

Italian bread

mixed salad leaves

tomato slices

method

1 Preheat the barbecue. Using a sharp knife, slice the aubergine into thin rounds.

2 Mix the lemon juice and olive oil together in a small bowl and season the mixture with salt and pepper to taste. Brush the aubergine slices with the olive oil and lemon juice mixture and cook over medium hot coals for 2–3 minutes, without turning, until golden on the under side.

3 Turn half of the aubergine slices over and sprinkle with cheese and chopped sun-dried tomatoes.

4 Place the remaining aubergine slices on top of the cheese and tomatoes, turning them so that the pale side is uppermost. Barbecue for 1–2 minutes, then carefully turn the whole sandwich over and barbecue for a further 1–2 minutes. Baste with the olive oil mixture.

5 Serve in Italian bread with mixed salad leaves and a few slices of tomato.

vegetarian sausages

ingredients

SERVES 4

1 tbsp sunflower oil, plus
	extra for oiling

1 small onion, finely chopped

50 g/1^3/$_4$ oz mushrooms,
	finely chopped

^{1}/$_2$ red pepper, deseeded and
	finely chopped

400 g/14 oz canned
	cannellini beans, rinsed
	and drained

100 g/3^1/$_2$ oz fresh
	breadcrumbs

100 g/3^1/$_2$ oz Cheddar
	cheese, grated

1 tsp dried mixed herbs

1 egg yolk

seasoned plain flour

to serve

fresh finger rolls

fried onion slices

tomato chutney

method

1 Heat the sunflower oil in a saucepan. Add the onion, mushrooms and pepper and fry until softened.

2 Mash the cannellini beans in a large bowl. Add the onion, mushroom and pepper mixture, the breadcrumbs, cheese, herbs and egg yolk and mix well. Press the mixture together with your fingers and shape into 8 sausages. Roll each sausage in the seasoned flour. Leave to chill in the refrigerator for at least 30 minutes.

3 Preheat the barbecue. Cook the sausages on a sheet of oiled foil set over medium–hot coals for 15–20 minutes, turning and basting frequently with oil, until golden. Split the finger rolls down the centre and insert a layer of fried onions. Place the sausages in the rolls and serve with tomato chutney.

cheese & vegetable-filled rolls

ingredients

SERVES 4

2 red peppers, deseeded and
    cut into quarters

2 courgettes, trimmed and
    sliced

1 large onion, cut into rings

150 g/5^1/$_2$ oz baby corn

3 tbsp olive oil

4 large white or wholemeal
    rolls, halved horizontally
    to make 8 thinner rounds

115 g/4 oz grated firm cheese

soured cream, to serve

method

1 Cook the peppers on the barbecue, skin side down, for 5 minutes or until the skins are charred. Transfer them to a polythene bag, seal the bag and set to one side. Brush the courgettes, onion rings and corn with oil and barbecue over hot coals for 5 minutes, turning them frequently and basting with more oil if necessary.

2 While the vegetables are on the barbecue, take the bottom halves of the rolls, brush the cut sides with oil and sprinkle over some cheese. Cover with the top halves, then wrap each bun in foil and transfer them to the barbecue. Warm for 2–4 minutes, just until the cheese starts to melt (do not overcook).

3 While the rolls are warming, take the pepper quarters from the bag and remove the skins. Chop the flesh into small pieces and transfer it to a plate with the other vegetables.

4 Transfer the rolls to serving plates and remove the foil. Fill them with the cooked vegetables and soured cream and serve at once.

something different

Everyone likes a change from time to time and if you're throwing a barbecue party, you may want to treat your guests to something a little different and more imaginative than usual. This doesn't have to mean spending a lot more money or even putting in a great deal more time in preparation.

Marinades make all the difference to foods cooked on the barbecue, whether meat or fish. They add a real depth of flavour, tenderize meat and help to prevent fish from drying out over the heat. They are also very quick and easy to prepare.

While no one is likely to quarrel with a simple but delicious grilled steak, why not try some more adventurous cuts of meat, such as rack of lamb or butterflied poussins? It's surprisingly easy to prepare these little chickens in this impressive way, but you can always ask your butcher to do it for you. Whole fish on the barbecue grill always looks striking – and tempting – even if they're only little silvery sardines.

For an extra-special and probably unexpected treat, serve a hot dessert. Many fruits are transformed by chargrilling. They also look fabulous threaded on to skewers and when stuffed or served with a luscious sauce, they simply melt in the mouth.

tabasco steaks with watercress butter

ingredients

SERVES 4

1 bunch of watercress

85 g/3 oz unsalted butter, softened

4 sirloin steaks, about 225 g/8 oz each

4 tsp Tabasco sauce

salt and pepper

method

1 Preheat the barbecue. Using a sharp knife, finely chop enough watercress to fill 4 tablespoons. Reserve a few watercress leaves for the garnish. Place the butter in a small bowl and beat in the chopped watercress with a fork until fully incorporated. Cover with clingfilm and leave to chill in the refrigerator until required. Sprinkle each steak with 1 teaspoon of the Tabasco sauce, rubbing it in well. Season to taste with salt and pepper.

2 Cook the steaks over hot coals for 2¹/₂ minutes each side for rare, 4 minutes each side for medium and 6 minutes each side for well done. Transfer to serving plates, garnish with the reserved watercress leaves and serve immediately, topped with the watercress butter.

beef with wild mushrooms

ingredients

SERVES 4

4 beef steaks

50 g/1¾ oz butter

1–2 garlic cloves, crushed

150 g/5½ oz mixed wild
mushrooms

2 tbsp chopped fresh parsley

to serve

salad leaves

cherry tomatoes, halved

method

1 Preheat the barbecue. Place the steaks on a chopping board and using a sharp knife, cut a pocket into the side of each steak.

2 To make the stuffing, heat the butter in a large frying pan. Add the garlic and fry gently for 1 minute. Add the mushrooms to the frying pan and sauté gently for 4–6 minutes, or until tender. Remove the frying pan from the heat and stir in the parsley.

3 Divide the mushroom mixture into 4 and insert a portion into the pocket of each steak. Seal the pocket with a cocktail stick. If preparing ahead, allow the mixture to cool before stuffing the steaks.

4 Cook the steaks over hot coals, searing the meat over the hottest part of the barbecue for 2 minutes on each side. Move the steaks to an area with slightly less intense heat and barbecue for a further 4–10 minutes on each side, depending on how well done you like your steaks.

5 Transfer the steaks to serving plates and remove the cocktail sticks. Serve with salad leaves and cherry tomatoes.

butterflied lamb with balsamic vinegar & mint

ingredients

SERVES 4

1 boned leg of lamb, about
    1.8 kg/4 lb
8 tbsp balsamic vinegar
grated rind and juice of
    1 lemon
150 ml/5 fl oz sunflower oil
4 tbsp chopped fresh mint
2 garlic cloves, crushed
2 tbsp light muscovado sugar
salt and pepper

to serve

barbecued vegetables, such
    as peppers and courgettes
black or green olives

method

1 Open out the boned leg of lamb so that its shape resembles a butterfly. Thread 2–3 skewers through the meat to make it easier to turn on the barbecue.

2 Mix the balsamic vinegar, lemon rind and juice, sunflower oil, mint, garlic, sugar and salt and pepper to taste together in a non-metallic dish that is large enough to hold the lamb. Place the lamb in the dish and turn it over a few times so that the meat is coated on both sides with the marinade. Cover and leave to marinate in the refrigerator for at least 6 hours, or preferably overnight, turning occasionally.

3 Preheat the barbecue. Remove the lamb from the marinade and reserve the liquid for basting. Place the rack about 15 cm/6 inches above the coals and cook the lamb for 30 minutes on each side, turning once and basting frequently with the marinade.

4 Transfer the lamb to a chopping board and remove the skewers. Cut the lamb into slices across the grain and serve with barbecued vegetables and olives.

rack of lamb

ingredients

SERVES 4

4 racks of lamb, each with
    4 cutlets
2 tbsp extra virgin olive oil
1 tbsp balsamic vinegar
1 tbsp lemon juice
3 tbsp finely chopped fresh
    rosemary
1 small onion, finely chopped
salt and pepper

method

1 Place the racks of lamb in a large, shallow, non-metallic dish. Place the oil, vinegar, lemon juice, rosemary and onion in a jug and stir together. Season to taste with salt and pepper.

2 Pour the marinade over the lamb and turn until thoroughly coated. Cover with clingfilm and leave to marinate in the refrigerator for 1 hour, turning occasionally.

3 Preheat the barbecue. Drain the racks of lamb, reserving the marinade. Cook over medium–hot coals, brushing frequently with the marinade, for 10 minutes on each side. Serve immediately.

caribbean pork

ingredients

SERVES 4

4 pork loin chops

4 tbsp dark muscovado sugar

4 tbsp orange or pineapple
juice

2 tbsp Jamaican rum

1 tbsp desiccated coconut

1/2 tsp ground cinnamon

mixed salad leaves, to serve

coconut rice

225 g/8 oz basmati rice

450 ml/16 fl oz water

150 ml/5 fl oz coconut milk

4 tbsp raisins

4 tbsp roasted peanuts
or cashew nuts

2 tbsp desiccated coconut,
toasted

salt and pepper

method

1 Trim any excess fat from the pork and place the chops in a shallow, non-metallic dish. Mix the sugar, fruit juice, rum, coconut and cinnamon together in a bowl, stirring until the sugar dissolves. Pour the mixture over the pork, cover and leave to marinate in the refrigerator for at least 2 hours, or preferably overnight.

2 Preheat the barbecue. Remove the pork from the marinade, reserving the liquid for basting. Cook over hot coals for 15–20 minutes, basting with the marinade.

3 Meanwhile, make the coconut rice. Rinse the rice under cold running water, place it in a saucepan with the water and coconut milk and bring gently to the boil. Stir, cover and reduce the heat. Simmer gently for 12 minutes, or until the rice is tender and the liquid has been absorbed. Fluff up with a fork.

4 Stir the raisins and nuts into the rice, season to taste with salt and pepper and sprinkle with the coconut. Transfer the pork and rice to warmed serving plates and serve immediately with mixed salad leaves.

lemon & herb pork escalopes

ingredients

SERVES 4

4 pork escalopes

2 tbsp sunflower oil

6 bay leaves, torn into pieces

grated rind and juice of
    2 lemons

125 ml/4 fl oz beer

1 tbsp clear honey

6 juniper berries, lightly
    crushed

1 crisp dessert apple

salt and pepper

method

1 Place the pork escalopes in a large, shallow, non-metallic dish. Heat the oil in a small, heavy-based saucepan. Add the bay leaves and stir-fry for 1 minute. Stir in the lemon rind and juice, beer, honey and juniper berries and season to taste with salt and pepper.

2 Pour the mixture over the pork, turning to coat. Cover with clingfilm, leave to cool, then leave to marinate in the refrigerator for up to 8 hours.

3 Preheat the barbecue. Drain the pork, reserving the marinade. Core the apple and cut into rings. Cook the pork over medium hot coals, brushing frequently with the reserved marinade, for 5 minutes on each side, or until thoroughly cooked. Cook the apples on the barbecue, brushing frequently with the marinade, for 3 minutes. Transfer the pork to a large serving plate with the apple rings and serve immediately.

tarragon turkey

ingredients

SERVES 4

4 turkey breasts, about
175 g/6 oz each

4 tsp wholegrain mustard

8 fresh tarragon sprigs,
plus extra to garnish

4 smoked back bacon
rashers

salt and pepper

salad leaves, to serve

method

1 Preheat the barbecue. Season the turkey to taste with salt and pepper, and, using a round-bladed knife, spread the mustard evenly over the turkey.

2 Place 2 tarragon sprigs on top of each turkey breast and wrap a bacon rasher around it to hold the herbs in place. Secure with a cocktail stick.

3 Cook the turkey over medium–hot coals for 5–8 minutes on each side. Transfer to serving plates and garnish with tarragon sprigs. Serve with salad leaves.

butterflied poussins

ingredients

SERVES 4

4 poussins, about 450 g/
    1 lb each

1 tbsp paprika

1 tbsp mustard powder

1 tbsp ground cumin

pinch of cayenne pepper

1 tbsp tomato ketchup

1 tbsp lemon juice

5 tbsp melted butter

salt

fresh coriander sprigs,
    to garnish

corn on the cob, to serve

method

1 To butterfly the poussins, turn 1 bird breast-side down and, using strong kitchen scissors or poultry shears, cut through the skin and ribcage along both sides of the backbone, from tail to neck. Remove the backbone and turn the bird breast-side up. Press down firmly on the breastbone to flatten. Fold the wingtips underneath. Push a skewer through one wing, the top of the breast and out of the other wing. Push a second skewer through one thigh, the bottom of the breast and out through the other thigh. Repeat with the remaining poussins.

2 Mix the paprika, mustard powder, cumin, cayenne, tomato ketchup and lemon juice together in a small bowl and season to taste with salt. Gradually stir in the butter to make a smooth paste. Spread the paste evenly over the poussins, cover and leave to marinate in the refrigerator for up to 8 hours.

3 Preheat the barbecue. Cook the poussins over medium–hot coals, turning frequently, for 25–30 minutes, brushing with a little oil if necessary. Transfer to a serving plate, garnish with fresh coriander sprigs and serve with corn on the cob.

fruity duck

ingredients

SERVES 4

4 duck breasts

115 g/4 oz ready-to-eat dried
apricots

2 shallots, thinly sliced

2 tbsp clear honey

1 tsp sesame oil

2 tsp Chinese five-spice
powder

method

1 Preheat the barbecue. Using a sharp knife, cut a long slit in the fleshy side of each duck breast to make a pocket. Divide the apricots and shallots between the pockets and secure with skewers.

2 Mix the honey and sesame oil together in a small bowl and brush all over the duck. Sprinkle with the Chinese five-spice powder.

3 Cook the duck over medium–hot coals for 6–8 minutes on each side. Remove the skewers, transfer to a large serving plate and serve immediately.

orange & lemon peppered monkfish

ingredients

SERVES 8

2 oranges

2 lemons

2 monkfish tails, about
    500 g/1 lb 2 oz each,
    skinned and cut into
    4 fillets

8 fresh lemon thyme sprigs

2 tbsp olive oil

2 tbsp green peppercorns,
    lightly crushed

salt

method

1 Cut 8 orange slices and 8 lemon slices, reserving the remaining fruit. Rinse the monkfish fillets under cold running water and pat dry with kitchen paper. Place the monkfish fillets, cut side up, on a work surface and divide the citrus slices among them. Top with the lemon thyme. Tie each fillet at intervals with kitchen string to secure the citrus slices and thyme. Place the monkfish in a large, shallow, non-metallic dish.

2 Squeeze the juice from the remaining fruit and mix with the olive oil in a jug. Season to taste with salt, then spoon the mixture over the fish. Cover with clingfilm and leave to marinate in the refrigerator for up to 1 hour, spooning the marinade over the fish tails once or twice.

3 Preheat the barbecue. Drain the monkfish tails, reserving the marinade. Sprinkle the crushed green peppercorns over the fish, pressing them in with your fingers. Cook the monkfish over medium–hot coals, turning and brushing frequently with the reserved marinade, for 20–25 minutes. Transfer to a chopping board, remove and discard the string and cut the monkfish tails into slices. Serve immediately.

chargrilled red snapper

ingredients

SERVES 4

4 banana leaves

2 limes

3 garlic cloves

4 red mullet, about
350 g/12 oz each

2 spring onions, thinly sliced

2.5-cm/1-inch piece fresh
ginger

1 onion, finely chopped

4$\frac{1}{2}$ tsp groundnut or corn oil

3 tbsp kecap manis or light
soy sauce

1 tsp ground coriander

1 tsp ground cumin

$\frac{1}{4}$ tsp ground cloves

$\frac{1}{4}$ tsp ground turmeric

method

1 Preheat the barbecue. If necessary, cut the banana leaves into 4 x 40-cm/16-inch squares, using a sharp knife or scissors. Thinly slice 1$\frac{1}{2}$ limes and 1 garlic clove. Clean and scale the fish, then rinse it inside and out under cold running water. Pat dry with kitchen paper. Using a sharp knife, make a series of deep diagonal slashes on the side of each fish, then insert the lime and garlic slices into the slashes. Place the fish on the banana leaf squares and sprinkle with the spring onions.

2 Finely chop the remaining garlic and squeeze the juice from the remaining lime half. Finely chop the ginger, then place the garlic in a bowl with the onion, ginger, oil, kecap manis, spices and lime juice and mix to a paste.

3 Spoon the paste into the fish cavities and spread it over the outside. Roll up the parcels and tie securely with string. Cook over medium–hot coals, turning occasionally, for 15–20 minutes. Serve.

prawns with citrus salsa

ingredients

SERVES 6

36 large, raw tiger prawns
2 tbsp finely chopped fresh
    coriander
pinch of cayenne pepper
3–4 tbsp corn oil
fresh coriander leaves,
    to garnish
lime wedges, to serve

salsa

1 orange
1 tart eating apple, peeled,
    quartered and cored
2 fresh red chillies, deseeded
    and chopped
1 garlic clove, chopped
8 fresh coriander sprigs
8 fresh mint sprigs
4 tbsp lime juice
salt and pepper

method

1 Preheat the barbecue. To make the salsa, peel the orange and cut into segments. Reserve any juice. Put the orange segments, apple quarters, chillies, garlic, coriander and mint into a food processor and process until smooth. With the motor running, add the lime juice through the feeder tube. Transfer the salsa to a serving bowl and season to taste with salt and pepper. Cover with clingfilm and leave to chill in the refrigerator until required.

2 Using a sharp knife, remove and discard the heads from the prawns, then peel off the shells. Cut along the back of the prawns and remove the dark intestinal vein. Rinse the prawns under cold running water and pat dry with kitchen paper. Mix the chopped coriander, cayenne and corn oil together in a dish. Add the prawns and toss well to coat.

3 Cook the prawns over medium–hot coals for 3 minutes on each side, or until they have changed colour. Transfer to a large serving plate, garnish with fresh coriander leaves and serve immediately with lime wedges and the salsa.

stuffed sardines

ingredients

SERVES 6

15 g/^{1}/$_2$ oz fresh parsley,
    finely chopped

4 garlic cloves, finely
    chopped

12 fresh sardines, cleaned
    and scaled

3 tbsp lemon juice

85 g/3 oz plain flour

1 tsp ground cumin

salt and pepper

olive oil, for brushing

method

1 Place the parsley and garlic in a bowl and mix together. Rinse the fish inside and out under cold running water and pat dry with kitchen paper. Spoon the herb mixture into the fish cavities and pat the remainder all over the outside of the fish. Sprinkle the sardines with lemon juice and transfer to a large, shallow, non-metallic dish. Cover with clingfilm and leave to marinate in the refrigerator for 1 hour.

2 Preheat the barbecue. Mix the flour and ground cumin together in a bowl, then season to taste with salt and pepper. Spread out the seasoned flour on a large plate and gently roll the sardines in the flour to coat.

3 Brush the sardines with olive oil and cook over medium hot coals for 3–4 minutes on each side. Serve immediately.

chargrilled devils

ingredients

SERVES 6

36 fresh oysters

18 streaky bacon rashers, rinded

1 tbsp mild paprika

1 tsp cayenne pepper

sauce

1 fresh red chilli, deseeded and finely chopped

1 garlic clove, finely chopped

1 shallot, finely chopped

2 tbsp finely chopped fresh parsley

2 tbsp lemon juice

salt and pepper

method

1 Preheat the barbecue. Open the oysters, catching the juice from the shells in a bowl. Cut the oysters from the bottom shells, reserve and tip any remaining juice into the bowl. To make the sauce, add the red chilli, garlic, shallot, parsley and lemon juice to the bowl, then season to taste with salt and pepper and mix well. Cover the bowl with clingfilm and leave to chill in the refrigerator until required.

2 Cut each bacon rasher in half across the centre. Season the oysters with paprika and cayenne, then roll each oyster up inside half a bacon rasher. Thread 6 wrapped oysters on to each of the 6 presoaked wooden skewers.

3 Cook over hot coals, turning frequently, for 5 minutes, or until the bacon is well browned and crispy. Transfer to a large serving plate and serve immediately with the sauce.

chocolate rum bananas

ingredients

SERVES 4

1 tbsp butter

225 g/8 oz plain or milk
chocolate

4 large bananas

2 tbsp rum

crème fraîche, mascarpone
cheese or ice cream,
to serve

grated nutmeg, to decorate

method

1 Take four 25-cm/10-inch squares of aluminium foil and brush them with butter.

2 Grate the chocolate. Make a careful slit lengthways in the peel of each banana, and open just wide enough to insert the chocolate. Place the grated chocolate inside the bananas, along their lengths, then close them up.

3 Wrap each stuffed banana in a square of foil, then barbecue them over hot coals for about 5–10 minutes, or until the chocolate has melted inside the bananas. Remove from the barbecue, place the bananas on individual serving plates and pour some rum into each banana.

4 Serve at once with crème fraîche, mascarpone cheese or ice cream, topped with nutmeg.

mascarpone peaches

ingredients

SERVES 4

4 peaches

175 g/6 oz mascarpone cheese

40 g/1¹/₂ oz pecan nuts or
    walnuts, chopped

1 tsp sunflower oil

4 tbsp maple syrup

method

1 Cut the peaches in half and remove the stones. If you are preparing this recipe in advance, press the peach halves together and wrap in clingfilm until required.

2 Mix the mascarpone cheese and pecans together in a bowl until well combined. Leave to chill in the refrigerator until required. Preheat the barbecue. Brush the peach halves with a little sunflower oil and place on a rack set over medium hot coals. Cook the peach halves for 5–10 minutes, turning once, until hot.

3 Transfer the peach halves to a serving dish and top with the mascarpone and nut mixture. Drizzle the maple syrup over the peaches and mascarpone filling and serve immediately.

tropical pineapple

ingredients

SERVES 4

1 pineapple

3 tbsp dark rum

2 tbsp muscovado sugar

1 tsp ground ginger

4 tbsp unsalted butter, melted

method

1 Preheat the barbecue. Using a sharp knife, cut off the crown of the pineapple, then cut the fruit into 2-cm/³/4-inch thick slices. Cut away the peel from each slice and flick out the 'eyes' with the point of the knife. Stamp out the cores with an apple corer or small pastry cutter.

2 Mix the rum, sugar, ginger and butter together in a jug, stirring constantly, until the sugar has dissolved. Brush the pineapple rings with the rum mixture.

3 Cook the pineapple rings over hot coals for 3–4 minutes on each side. Transfer to serving plates and serve immediately with the remaining rum mixture poured over them.

stuffed figs

ingredients

SERVES 4

8 fresh figs
100 g/3^1/$_2$ oz cream cheese
1 tsp powdered cinnamon
3 tbsp brown sugar
natural yogurt, crème fraîche,
    mascarpone cheese or
    ice cream, to serve

method

1 Cut out eight 18-cm/7-inch squares of aluminium foil. Make a deep cross in each fig, then place each fig on a square of foil.

2 Put the cream cheese in a bowl. Add the cinnamon and stir until well combined. Stuff the inside of each fig with the cinnamon cream cheese, then sprinkle a teaspoon of sugar over each one. Close the foil around each fig to make a parcel.

3 Place the parcels on the barbecue and cook over hot coals, turning them frequently, for about 10 minutes, or until the figs are cooked to your taste.

4 Transfer the figs to serving plates and serve at once with natural yogurt, crème fraîche, mascarpone cheese or ice cream.

mixed fruit kebabs

ingredients

SERVES 4

2 nectarines, halved and
    stoned

2 kiwi fruit

4 red plums

1 mango, peeled, halved
    and stoned

2 bananas, peeled and
    thickly sliced

8 strawberries, hulled

1 tbsp clear honey

3 tbsp Cointreau

method

1 Cut the nectarine halves into wedges and place in a large, shallow dish. Peel and quarter the kiwi fruit. Cut the plums in half and remove the stones. Cut the mango flesh into chunks and add to the dish with the kiwi fruit, plums, bananas and strawberries.

2 Mix the honey and Cointreau together in a jug until well blended. Pour the mixture over the fruit and toss lightly to coat. Cover with clingfilm and leave to marinate in the refrigerator for 1 hour.

3 Preheat the barbecue. Drain the fruit, reserving the marinade. Thread the fruit on to several presoaked wooden skewers and cook over medium–hot coals, turning and brushing frequently with the reserved marinade, for 5–7 minutes, then serve.

toffee fruit kebabs

ingredients

SERVES 4

2 dessert apples, cored and
   cut into wedges

2 firm pears, cored and
   cut into wedges

juice of $^1/_2$ lemon

25 g/1 oz light muscovado
   sugar

$^1/_4$ tsp ground allspice

25 g/1 oz unsalted butter,
   melted

sauce

125 g/4$^1/_2$ oz butter

100 g/3$^1/_2$ oz light
   muscovado sugar

6 tbsp double cream

method

1 Preheat the barbecue. Toss the apples
and pears in the lemon juice to prevent any
discoloration.

2 Mix the sugar and allspice together and
sprinkle over the fruit. Thread the fruit pieces
on to skewers.

3 To make the toffee sauce, place the butter
and sugar in a saucepan and heat, stirring
gently, until the butter has melted and the
sugar has dissolved. Add the cream to the
saucepan and bring to the boil. Boil for
1–2 minutes, then leave to cool slightly.

4 Meanwhile, place the fruit kebabs over hot
coals and cook for 5 minutes, turning and
basting frequently with the melted butter, until
the fruit is just tender. Transfer the fruit kebabs
to warmed serving plates and serve with the
cooled toffee sauce.

skewers

Whether they're called kebabs, brochettes or any other name, bite-sized pieces of meat, fish and vegetables threaded on to skewers and sizzling on the barbecue grill always look appetizing and appealing. They are ideal for entertaining as they seem rather special and, although they can be time consuming to prepare, they cook very quickly. This is especially helpful if your barbecue isn't very big and you have a lot of guests. Children absolutely love kebabs but make sure that you transfer the food for them before serving it as you don't want small mouths burnt on hot metal or tongues impaled on the pointed ends of skewers.

Prawns are 'custom-made' for kebabs and cubes of meaty fish, such as swordfish, cheese, firm tofu and vegetables are also ideal because they taste best when cooked quickly. Use good-quality cuts of meat, such as sirloin, fillet and chicken breast, and cut them into equal-size cubes. If they are threaded alternately with vegetables or mushrooms, try to make sure that these are the same size too and don't pack them too tightly or too close to the ends of the skewers.

If you soak bamboo or wooden skewers in cold water for 30 minutes before you use them, this helps to reduce the chances of their charring during cooking.

beef teriyaki

ingredients

SERVES 4

450 g/1 lb extra thin beef
    steaks
1 yellow pepper, deseeded
    and cut into chunks
8 spring onions, trimmed and
    cut into short lengths
salad leaves, to serve

sauce

1 tsp cornflour
2 tbsp dry sherry
2 tbsp white wine vinegar
3 tbsp soy sauce
1 tbsp dark muscovado sugar
1 garlic clove, crushed
$^{1}/_{2}$ tsp ground cinnamon
$^{1}/_{2}$ tsp ground ginger

method

1 Place the beef steaks in a shallow, non-metallic dish. To make the sauce, mix the cornflour and sherry together in a small bowl, then stir in the remaining sauce ingredients. Pour the sauce over the meat, cover with clingfilm and leave to marinate in the refrigerator for at least 2 hours.

2 Preheat the barbecue. Remove the meat from the sauce and reserve. Pour the sauce into a small saucepan and boil for at least 5 minutes, stirring occasionally.

3 Cut the meat into thin strips and thread these, concertina-style, on to several presoaked wooden skewers, alternating each strip of meat with the pieces of pepper and spring onion. Cook the kebabs over hot coals for 5–8 minutes, turning and basting the beef and vegetables occasionally with the reserved sauce.

4 Arrange the skewers on serving plates and pour over the remaining sauce. Serve with salad leaves.

surf 'n' turf skewers

ingredients

SERVES 2

225 g/8 oz fillet steak, about
    2.5-cm/1-inch thick
8 raw unpeeled tiger prawns
4 tbsp butter
2 garlic cloves, crushed
3 tbsp chopped fresh parsley,
    plus extra parsley sprigs,
    to garnish
finely grated rind and juice of
    1 lime
olive oil, for oiling
salt and pepper
lime wedges, to garnish
crusty bread, to serve

method

1 Cut the steak into 2.5-cm/1-inch cubes. To prepare the prawns, use your fingers to pull off their heads, then peel off their shells, leaving the tails on. Using a sharp knife, make a shallow slit along the back of each prawn, then pull out the dark vein and discard. Rinse the prawns under cold running water and dry well on kitchen paper.

2 Thread an equal number of the steak cubes and prawns on to 2 oiled metal kebab skewers or presoaked wooden skewers. Season the kebabs to taste with pepper.

3 Preheat the barbecue. Meanwhile, put the butter and garlic into a small saucepan and heat gently until melted. Remove from the heat and add the parsley, lime rind and juice and salt and pepper to taste. Leave in a warm place so that the butter remains melted.

4 Brush the kebabs with a little of the melted butter. Put the kebabs on to an oiled grill rack and cook over hot coals for 4–8 minutes until the steak is cooked according to your taste and the prawns turn pink, turning the kebabs frequently during cooking, and brushing with the remaining melted butter.

5 Serve the kebabs hot on the skewers, with the remaining butter spooned over. Garnish with lime wedges and parsley sprigs and serve with crusty bread to mop up the buttery juice.

pork & apple brochettes

ingredients

SERVES 4

450 g/1 lb pork fillet

300 ml/10 fl oz dry cider

1 tbsp finely chopped fresh
    sage

6 black peppercorns, crushed

2 crisp eating apples

1 tbsp sunflower oil

crusty bread, to serve

method

1 Using a sharp knife, cut the pork into 2.5-cm/1-inch cubes, then place in a large, shallow, non-metallic dish. Mix the cider, sage and peppercorns together in a jug, pour the mixture over the pork and turn until thoroughly coated. Cover with clingfilm and leave to marinate in the refrigerator for 1–2 hours.

2 Preheat the barbecue. Drain the pork, reserving the marinade. Core the apples, but do not peel, then cut into wedges. Dip the apple wedges into the reserved marinade and thread on to several metal skewers, alternating with the cubes of pork. Stir the sunflower oil into the remaining marinade.

3 Cook the brochettes over medium–hot coals, turning and brushing frequently with the reserved marinade, for 12–15 minutes. Transfer to a large serving plate and if you prefer, remove the meat and apples from the skewers before serving. Serve immediately with crusty bread.

pork & sage kebabs

ingredients

SERVES 4

450 g/1 lb pork mince

25 g/1 oz fresh breadcrumbs

1 small onion, chopped very
    finely

1 tbsp fresh sage, chopped

2 tbsp apple sauce

1/4 tsp ground nutmeg

salt and pepper

baste

3 tbsp olive oil

1 tbsp lemon juice

to serve

4 small pitta breads

mixed salad leaves

6 tbsp thick, natural yogurt

method

1 Place the mince in a mixing bowl together with the breadcrumbs, onion, sage, apple sauce, nutmeg and salt and pepper to taste. Mix until the ingredients are well combined. Using your hands, shape the mixture into small balls, about the size of large marbles, and leave to chill in the refrigerator for at least 30 minutes.

2 Meanwhile, soak several small wooden skewers in cold water for at least 30 minutes. Thread the meatballs on to the skewers.

3 To make the baste, mix together the oil and lemon juice in a small bowl, whisking with a fork until it is well blended.

4 Barbecue the kebabs over hot coals for 8–10 minutes, turning and basting frequently with the lemon and oil mixture, until the meat is golden and cooked through. Line the pitta breads with the salad leaves and spoon over some of the yogurt. Serve with the kebabs.

shish kebabs

ingredients

SERVES 4–6

500 g/1 lb 2 oz boneless leg
or neck of lamb with a
small amount of fat, cut
into 2-cm/³/₄-inch cubes

2 green peppers, halved,
deseeded and cut into
2-cm/³/₄-inch pieces

1 onion, quartered and
separated into layers

2 cherry tomatoes per skewer

marinade

2 tbsp milk

2 tbsp olive oil, plus extra for
oiling

1 large onion, grated

1 tbsp tomato purée

¹/₂ tsp ground cumin

coarse sea salt and pepper

to serve

lemon wedges

warmed pitta bread (optional)

tzatziki

method

1 To make the marinade, put all the ingredients in a bowl and stir until the tomato purée is evenly dispersed. Add the lamb cubes and use your hands to coat well with the marinade. Cover and leave to marinate in the refrigerator for 2 hours. If you are using wooden skewers, soak them in cold water for at least 1 hour.

2 Heat a ridged, cast-iron griddle pan over a very high heat or preheat the grill to its highest setting. Alternatively, light a barbecue and leave to burn until the flames die down and the coals are glowing. Lightly brush presoaked wooden or long, flat metal skewers with oil, then thread an equal quantity of the lamb cubes onto each one, occasionally interspersing with green pepper pieces, onion layers and the tomatoes. Sprinkle with sea salt.

3 Preheat the barbecue. Add the kebabs and cook, turning frequently and basting with the remaining marinade, for 8–10 minutes, or until the lamb and peppers are charred on the edges. Cut one lamb cube open to check that the meat is cooked to your liking.

4 Serve immediately with lemon wedges for squeezing over, warmed pitta bread, if using, and tzatziki.

indian kofta

ingredients

SERVES 4

1 small onion
450 g/1 lb fresh lean lamb
 mince
2 tbsp curry paste
2 tbsp natural yogurt
sunflower oil, for basting

tomato sambal
3 tomatoes, deseeded and
 diced
pinch of ground coriander
pinch of ground cumin
2 tsp chopped fresh
 coriander
salt and pepper

to serve
poppadoms
chutney

method

1 Place the onion in a food processor and chop finely. Add the lamb and process briefly to chop the mince further. Alternatively, grate the onion finely before mixing it with the lamb.

2 Add the curry paste and yogurt and mix well. Divide the mixture into 8 equal-sized portions. Press and shape the mixture into 8 sausage shapes and push each one on to a metal or presoaked wooden skewer, pressing the mixture together firmly so that it holds its shape. Leave to chill in the refrigerator for at least 30 minutes, or until required.

3 To make the tomato sambal, mix the tomatoes, spices, chopped coriander and salt and pepper to taste together in a bowl. Leave to stand for at least 30 minutes for the flavours to combine.

4 Preheat the barbecue. Cook the kebabs on an oiled rack over hot coals for 10–15 minutes, turning frequently. Baste with a little sunflower oil if required. Serve accompanied with poppadoms, chutney and the tomato sambal.

shashlik

ingredients

SERVES 4

675 g/1 lb 8 oz boneless
    leg of lamb, cut into
    2.5-cm/1-inch cubes
12 large mushrooms
4 streaky bacon rashers,
    rinded
8 cherry tomatoes
1 large green pepper,
    deseeded and cut into
    squares
crusty bread, to serve

marinade

4 tbsp sunflower oil
4 tbsp lemon juice
1 onion, finely chopped
1/2 tsp dried rosemary
1/2 tsp dried thyme
salt and pepper

method

1 Place the lamb and mushrooms in a large, shallow, non-metallic dish. Mix all the ingredients for the marinade together in a jug, seasoning to taste with salt and pepper. Pour the mixture over the lamb and mushrooms, turning to coat. Cover with clingfilm and leave to marinate in the refrigerator for up to 8 hours.

2 Preheat the barbecue. Cut the bacon rashers in half across the centre and stretch with a heavy, flat-bladed knife, then roll up. Drain the lamb and mushrooms, reserving the marinade. Thread the bacon rolls, lamb, mushrooms, tomatoes and green pepper squares alternately on to metal skewers. Sieve the marinade.

3 Cook the kebabs over medium–hot coals, turning and brushing frequently with the reserved marinade, for 10–15 minutes. Transfer to a large serving plate and serve immediately with crusty bread.

marinated lamb & vegetable kebabs

ingredients

SERVES 4

juice of 2 large lemons

100 ml/3^1/$_2$ fl oz olive oil

1 garlic clove, crushed

1 tbsp chopped fresh oregano
or mint

700 g/1 lb 9 oz boned leg or
fillet of lamb

2 green peppers, halved,
deseeded and cut into
3-cm/1^1/$_4$-inch cubes

2 courgettes, cut into 2.5-cm/
1-inch pieces

12 button onions

8 large bay leaves

salt and pepper

freshly cooked rice, to serve

lemon wedges, to garnish

tzatziki, to serve

method

1 Put the lemon juice, oil, garlic, oregano, salt and pepper in a bowl and whisk together. Trim and cut the lamb into 4-cm/1^1/$_2$-inch cubes and add to the marinade.

2 Toss the lamb in the marinade, cover and leave in the fridge overnight or for at least 8 hours. Stir occasionally to coat the lamb.

3 When ready to serve, thread the lamb, peppers, courgettes, onions and bay leaves onto 8 flat, greased metal kebab skewers, alternating and dividing the ingredients as evenly as possible. Place on a greased grill pan.

4 Preheat the grill then put the kebabs under the grill for 10–15 minutes, turning frequently and basting with any remaining marinade, until cooked. Serve hot, on a bed of rice with lemon wedges and a bowl of tzatziki.

chicken satay

ingredients

SERVES 4

8 tbsp crunchy peanut butter

1 onion, roughly chopped

1 garlic clove, roughly
    chopped

2 tbsp creamed coconut

4 tbsp groundnut oil

1 tsp light soy sauce

2 tbsp lime juice

2 fresh red chillies, deseeded
    and chopped

3 kaffir lime leaves, torn

4 skinless, boneless chicken
    breasts, about 175 g/6 oz
    each, cut into 2.5-cm/
    1-inch cubes

method

1 Put the peanut butter, onion, garlic, coconut, groundnut oil, soy sauce, lime juice, chillies and lime leaves into a food processor and process to a smooth paste. Transfer the paste to a large glass bowl.

2 Add the chicken cubes to the dish and stir to coat thoroughly. Cover with clingfilm and leave to marinate in the refrigerator for up to 8 hours.

3 Preheat the barbecue. Thread the chicken cubes on to several presoaked wooden skewers, reserving the marinade. Cook the skewers over medium–hot coals, turning and brushing frequently with the marinade, for 10 minutes, or until thoroughly cooked. Transfer to a large serving plate and serve immediately.

chicken kebabs with yogurt sauce

ingredients

SERVES 4

300 ml/10 fl oz pint authentic
    Greek yogurt
2 garlic cloves, crushed
juice of $1/2$ lemon
1 tbsp chopped fresh herbs
    such as oregano, dill,
    tarragon or parsley

yogurt sauce

4 large skinned, boned
    chicken breasts
8 firm stalks of fresh
    rosemary, optional
corn oil, for brushing
salt and pepper

rice, to serve
shredded Cos lettuce,
    to serve
lemon wedges, to garnish

method

1 To make the sauce, put the yogurt, garlic, lemon juice, oregano, salt and pepper in a large bowl and mix well together.

2 Cut the chicken breasts into chunks measuring about 4 cm/$1\,1/2$ inches square. Add to the yogurt mixture and toss well together until the chicken pieces are coated. Cover and leave to marinate in the refrigerator for about 1 hour.

3 Preheat the barbecue. Thread the pieces of chicken onto 8 flat, greased, metal kebab skewers, presoaked wooden skewers or rosemary stalks and place on a greased grill pan.

4 Cook the kebabs over hot coals for about 15 minutes, turning and basting with the remaining marinade occasionally, until lightly browned and tender.

5 Pour the remaining marinade into a saucepan and heat gently but do not boil. Serve the kebabs on a bed of rice topped with shredded lettuce and garnish with lemon wedges. Accompany with the yogurt sauce.

zesty kebabs

ingredients

SERVES 4

4 skinless, boneless chicken
breasts, about 175 g/
6 oz each
finely grated rind and juice of
1/2 lemon
finely grated rind and juice of
1/2 orange
2 tbsp clear honey
2 tbsp olive oil
2 tbsp chopped fresh mint,
plus extra to garnish
1/4 tsp ground coriander
salt and pepper
citrus zest, to garnish

method

1 Using a sharp knife, cut the chicken into
2.5-cm/1-inch cubes, then place them in a
large glass bowl. Place the lemon and orange
rind, the lemon and orange juice, the honey,
oil, mint and ground coriander in a jug and
mix together. Season to taste with salt and
pepper. Pour the marinade over the chicken
cubes and toss until they are thoroughly
coated. Cover with clingfilm and leave to
marinate in the refrigerator for up to 8 hours.

2 Preheat the barbecue. Drain the chicken
cubes, reserving the marinade. Thread the
chicken on to several long metal skewers.

3 Cook the skewers over medium–hot coals,
turning and brushing frequently with the
reserved marinade, for 6–10 minutes, or until
thoroughly cooked. Transfer to a large serving
plate, garnish with fresh chopped mint and
citrus zest and serve immediately.

italian devilled chicken

ingredients

SERVES 4

4 skinless, boneless chicken
    breasts, about 175 g/6 oz
    each, cut into 2.5-cm/
    1-inch cubes

125 ml/4 fl oz olive oil

finely grated rind and juice of
    1 lemon

2 garlic cloves, finely
    chopped

2 tsp finely chopped dried red
    chillies

salt and pepper

fresh flat-leaf parsley sprigs,
    to garnish

method

1 Place the chicken cubes in a large, shallow, non-metallic dish. Place the olive oil, lemon rind and juice, garlic and chillies in a jug and stir together until well blended. Season to taste with salt and pepper.

2 Pour the mixture over the chicken and stir gently to coat. Cover with clingfilm and leave to marinate in the refrigerator for up to 8 hours.

3 Preheat the barbecue. Drain the chicken, reserving the marinade. Thread the chicken on to several presoaked wooden skewers and cook over medium–hot coals, turning and brushing frequently with the reserved marinade, for 6–10 minutes, or until thoroughly cooked. Transfer to a large serving dish, garnish with parsley sprigs and serve immediately.

turkey skewers with coriander pesto

ingredients

SERVES 4

450 g/1 lb skinless, boneless
    turkey, cut into 5-cm/
    2-inch cubes
2 courgettes, thickly sliced
1 red and 1 yellow pepper,
    deseeded and cut into
    5-cm/2-inch squares
8 cherry tomatoes
8 baby onions, peeled but left
    whole

marinade

6 tbsp olive oil
3 tbsp dry white wine
1 tsp green peppercorns,
    crushed
2 tbsp chopped fresh coriander
salt

coriander pesto

55 g/2 oz fresh coriander
    leaves
15 g/^{1}/$_2$ oz fresh parsley leaves
1 garlic clove
55 g/2 oz pine kernels
25 g/1 oz freshly grated
    Parmesan cheese
6 tbsp extra virgin olive oil
juice of 1 lemon

method

1 Place the turkey in a large glass bowl. To make the marinade, mix the olive oil, wine, peppercorns and coriander together in a jug and season to taste with salt. Pour the mixture over the turkey and turn until the turkey is thoroughly coated. Cover with clingfilm and leave to marinate in the refrigerator for 2 hours.

2 Preheat the barbecue. To make the pesto, put the coriander and parsley into a food processor and process until finely chopped. Add the garlic and pine kernels and pulse until chopped. Add the Parmesan cheese, oil and lemon juice and process briefly to mix. Transfer to a bowl, cover and leave to chill in the refrigerator until required.

3 Drain the turkey, reserving the marinade. Thread the turkey, courgette slices, pepper pieces, cherry tomatoes and onions alternately on to metal skewers. Cook over medium–hot coals, turning and brushing frequently with the marinade, for 10 minutes. Serve immediately with the coriander pesto.

spicy turkey & sausage kebabs

ingredients

MAKES 8

6 tbsp olive oil

2 garlic cloves, crushed

1 fresh red chilli, deseeded
     and chopped

350 g/12 oz turkey breast
     fillet

300 g/10 1/2 oz chorizo
     sausage

1 dessert apple

1 tbsp lemon juice

8 bay leaves

salt and pepper

method

1 Place the olive oil, garlic, chilli and salt and pepper to taste in a small screw-top jar and shake well to combine. Leave to stand for 1 hour for the garlic and chilli to flavour the oil.

2 Preheat the barbecue. Using a sharp knife, cut the turkey into 2.5-cm/1-inch pieces. Cut the sausage into 2.5-cm/1-inch lengths. Cut the apple into chunks and remove the core. Toss the apple in the lemon juice to prevent discoloration.

3 Thread the turkey and sausage pieces on to 8 metal skewers, alternating with the apple chunks and bay leaves.

4 Cook the kebabs over hot coals for 15 minutes, or until the turkey is cooked through. Turn and baste the kebabs frequently with the flavoured oil.

5 Transfer the kebabs to warmed serving plates and serve immediately.

caribbean fish kebabs

ingredients

SERVES 6

1 kg/2 lb 4 oz swordfish
    steaks
3 tbsp olive oil
3 tbsp lime juice
1 garlic clove, finely chopped
1 tsp paprika
3 onions, cut into wedges
6 tomatoes, cut into wedges
salt and pepper

method

1 Using a sharp knife, cut the fish into 2.5-cm/1-inch cubes and place in a shallow, non-metallic dish. Place the oil, lime juice, garlic and paprika in a jug and mix well. Season to taste with salt and pepper. Pour the marinade over the fish, turning to coat. Cover with clingfilm and leave to marinate in the refrigerator for 1 hour.

2 Preheat the barbecue. Thread the fish cubes, onion wedges and tomato wedges alternately on to 6 long, presoaked wooden skewers. Reserve the marinade.

3 Cook the kebabs over medium–hot coals for 8–10 minutes, turning and brushing frequently with the reserved marinade. When they are cooked through, transfer the kebabs to a large serving plate and serve immediately.

coconut prawns

ingredients

SERVES 4

6 spring onions

400 ml/14 fl oz coconut milk

finely grated rind and juice of
    1 lime

4 tbsp chopped fresh
    coriander, plus extra
    to garnish

2 tbsp corn or sunflower oil

650 g/1 lb 7 oz raw tiger
    prawns

pepper

lemon wedges, to garnish

method

1 Finely chop the spring onions and place in a large, shallow, non-metallic dish with the coconut milk, lime rind and juice, coriander and oil. Mix well and season to taste with pepper. Add the prawns, turning to coat. Cover with clingfilm and leave to marinate in the refrigerator for 1 hour.

2 Preheat the barbecue. Drain the prawns, reserving the marinade. Thread the prawns on to 8 long metal skewers.

3 Cook the skewers over medium–hot coals, brushing with the reserved marinade and turning frequently, for 8 minutes, or until they have changed colour. Serve the prawns immediately, garnished with the lemon wedges and chopped coriander.

chargrilled tuna & vegetable kebabs

ingredients

SERVES 4

4 tuna steaks, about
    140 g/5 oz each
2 red onions
12 cherry tomatoes
1 red pepper, deseeded and
    diced into 2.5-cm/1-inch
    pieces
1 yellow pepper, deseeded
    and diced into 2.5-cm/
    1-inch pieces
1 courgette, sliced
1 tbsp chopped fresh oregano
4 tbsp olive oil
freshly ground black pepper
lime wedges, to garnish
salad greens, to serve

method

1 Preheat the barbecue. Cut the tuna into 2.5-cm/1-inch dice. Peel the onions and cut each onion lengthways into 6 wedges.

2 Divide the fish and vegetables evenly between 8 presoaked wooden skewers and set aside. Mix the oregano and oil together in a small bowl. Season with salt and pepper and lightly brush the kebabs with the oil.

3 Cook the kebabs over hot coals for 10–15 minutes, or until evenly cooked, turning occasionally.

4 Garnish with lime wedges and serve with the salad greens.

monkfish & prawns kebabs

ingredients

SERVES 4

600 g/1 lb 5 oz monkfish

1 green pepper

1 onion

3 tbsp olive oil

3 tbsp lemon juice

2 garlic cloves, crushed

16 large fresh prawns, peeled

16 fresh bay leaves

salt and pepper

method

1 Cut the monkfish into chunks measuring about 2.5 cm/1 inch. Cut the pepper into similar sized chunks, discarding the core and seeds. Cut the onion into 6 wedges then cut each wedge in half widthways and separate the layers.

2 To make the marinade, put the oil, lemon juice, garlic, and salt and pepper to taste in a bowl and whisk together. Add the monkfish, prawns, onion and pepper pieces and toss together until coated in the marinade. Cover and leave to marinate in the fridge for 2–3 hours.

3 Thread the pieces of fish, pepper, onion and bay leaves onto 8 greased, flat metal kebab skewers, alternating and dividing the ingredients as evenly as possible. Place on a greased grill pan.

4 Preheat the barbecue. Cook the kebabs on an oiled rack over hot coals for 10–15 minutes, turning frequently and basting with any remaining marinade, until cooked and lightly charred. Serve hot.

swordfish kebabs

ingredients

SERVES 4

600 g/1 lb 5 oz boneless
    swordfish steaks, about
    2.5 cm/1 inch thick and
    cut into 2.5-cm/1-inch
    cubes
20 fresh bay leaves
olive oil, for oiling

marinade

4 tbsp extra virgin olive oil
2 tbsp freshly squeezed
    lemon juice
1 garlic clove, crushed to a
    paste with $1/4$ tsp salt
$1/4$ tsp white pepper
pinch of hot or smoked
    paprika, to taste
1 onion, halved and then cut
    into half-moon shapes
4 fresh bay leaves, torn in half

dressing

5 tbsp extra virgin olive oil
5 tbsp freshly squeezed
    lemon juice
2 tbsp chopped fresh dill

method

1 To make the marinade, whisk the oil, lemon juice, garlic, pepper and paprika together in a non-metallic bowl. Add the swordfish cubes and use your hands to coat gently with the marinade. Scatter the onion and torn bay leaves over the top. Cover and leave to marinate in the refrigerator for at least 4 hours.

2 Meanwhile, make the dressing. Whisk all the ingredients together in a small bowl, cover and set aside.

3 Put the whole bay leaves in a heatproof bowl, pour over enough boiling water to cover and leave to soften for 1 hour. Drain well and pat dry.

4 Preheat the barbecue. Lightly brush 4 long, flat metal skewers with oil and thread an equal quantity of the swordfish cubes and 5 bay leaves onto each. Cook the kebabs on an oiled rack over hot coals for 10–15 minutes, turning frequently and basting with any remaining marinade, until the swordfish feels firm. Discard the bay leaves before eating and serve the swordfish with the dressing.

greek vegetable kebabs

ingredients

SERVES 4

2 onions

8 new potatoes, washed but
    not peeled

1 aubergine, cut into 8 pieces

8 thick slices cucumber

1 red pepper, deseeded and
    cut into 8 pieces

1 yellow pepper, deseeded
    and cut into 8 pieces

225 g/8 oz halloumi cheese,
    cut into 8 cubes

2 nectarines, stoned and cut
    into wedges

8 button mushrooms

2 tbsp olive oil

2 tsp chopped fresh thyme

2 tsp chopped fresh rosemary

salt

tzatziki, to serve

method

1 Preheat the barbecue. Cut the onions into wedges, then place the onions and potatoes in a saucepan of lightly salted boiling water and cook for 20 minutes, or until just tender. Drain and leave to cool. Meanwhile, blanch the aubergine in boiling water for 2 minutes, then add the cucumber and simmer for 1 minute. Add the peppers and simmer for a further 2 minutes, then drain and leave the vegetables to cool.

2 Place the cooled vegetables, cheese, nectarines and mushrooms in a bowl. Add the olive oil and herbs and toss to coat. Thread the vegetables, cheese, nectarines and mushrooms on to several metal skewers.

3 Cook the kebabs over hot coals, turning frequently, for 15 minutes. Transfer to a large serving plate and serve immediately with tzatziki.

vegetable brochettes

ingredients

SERVES 4

2 courgettes

1 yellow pepper, deseeded
    and quartered

225 g/8 oz firm tofu (drained
    weight)

4 cherry tomatoes

4 baby onions

8 button mushrooms

honey glaze

2 tbsp olive oil

1 tbsp mustard

1 tbsp clear honey

salt and pepper

method

1 Preheat the barbecue. Using a vegetable peeler, peel off strips of skin along the length of the courgettes to leave alternate yellow and green stripes, then cut each courgette into 8 thick slices. Cut each of the yellow pepper quarters in half. Cut the drained tofu into 2.5-cm/1-inch cubes.

2 Thread the pieces of pepper, courgette slices, tofu cubes, cherry tomatoes, baby onions and button mushrooms on to 4 metal skewers.

3 To make the glaze, mix the olive oil, mustard and honey together in a jug and season to taste with salt and pepper.

4 Brush the brochettes with the honey glaze and cook over medium–hot coals, turning and brushing frequently with the glaze, for 8–10 minutes. Serve.

marinated tofu skewers

ingredients

SERVES 4

350 g/12 oz firm tofu
1 red pepper
1 yellow pepper
2 courgettes
8 button mushrooms

marinade

grated rind and juice of
$^{1}/_{2}$ lemon
1 garlic clove, crushed
$^{1}/_{2}$ tsp chopped fresh
rosemary
$^{1}/_{2}$ tsp chopped fresh thyme
1 tbsp walnut oil

to garnish

shredded carrot
lemon wedges

method

1 To make the marinade, mix the lemon rind and juice, garlic, rosemary, thyme and walnut oil together in a shallow dish. Drain the tofu, pat it dry on kitchen paper and cut it into squares. Add to the marinade and toss to coat. Leave to marinate for 20–30 minutes.

2 Preheat the barbecue. Deseed the peppers and cut into 2.5-cm/1-inch pieces. Blanch in boiling water for 4 minutes, refresh in cold water and drain. Using a vegetable peeler, remove strips of peel from the courgettes. Cut the courgettes into 2.5-cm/1-inch chunks.

3 Remove the tofu from the marinade, reserving the liquid for basting. Thread the tofu on to 8 presoaked wooden skewers, alternating with the peppers, courgette and button mushrooms.

4 Cook the skewers over medium–hot coals for 6 minutes, turning and basting with the marinade. Transfer the skewers to warmed serving plates, garnish with shredded carrot and lemon wedges and serve.

spicy caribbean kebabs

ingredients

SERVES 4

1 corn cob

1 ripe plantain, peeled and
        cut into thick slices

1 aubergine, cut into chunks

1 red pepper, deseeded and
        cut into chunks

1 green pepper, deseeded
        and cut into chunks

1 onion, cut into wedges

8 button mushrooms

4 cherry tomatoes

marinade

150 ml/5 fl oz tomato juice

4 tbsp sunflower oil

4 tbsp lime juice

3 tbsp dark soy sauce

1 shallot, finely chopped

2 garlic cloves, finely
        chopped

1 fresh green chilli, deseeded
        and finely chopped

1/2 tsp ground cinnamon

pepper

method

1 Using a sharp knife, remove the husks and silks from the corn cob and cut into 2.5-cm/ 1-inch thick slices.

2 Mix all the marinade ingredients together in a jug, seasoning to taste with pepper. Pour the marinade over the vegetables, tossing to coat. Cover with clingfilm and leave to marinate in the refrigerator for 3 hours.

3 Preheat the barbecue. Drain the vegetables, reserving the marinade. Thread the vegetables on to several metal skewers. Cook over hot coals, turning and brushing frequently with the reserved marinade, for 10–15 minutes. Transfer to a large serving plate and serve immediately.

cheese & red onion kebabs

ingredients

SERVES 4

3 red onions

450 g/1 lb halloumi cheese,
    cut into 2.5-cm/1-inch
    cubes

2 tart apples, cored and cut
    into wedges

4 tbsp olive oil

1 tbsp cider vinegar

1 tbsp Dijon mustard

1 garlic clove, finely chopped

1 tsp finely chopped sage

salt and pepper

method

1 Cut the onions into wedges, then place in a large, shallow, non-metallic dish with the cheese and apples. Mix the oil, vinegar, mustard, garlic and sage together in a jug and season to taste with salt and pepper.

2 Pour the marinade over the onions, cheese and apples, tossing to coat. Cover with clingfilm and leave to marinate in the refrigerator for 2 hours.

3 Preheat the barbecue. Drain the onions, cheese and apples, reserving the marinade. Thread the onions, cheese and apples alternately on to several metal skewers. Cook over hot coals, turning and brushing frequently with the reserved marinade, for 10–15 minutes. Transfer to a large serving plate and serve immediately.

on the side

While most attention is focused on what happens centre-stage on the grill, for a really successful barbecue, it is important to give some thought to side dishes, sauces and relishes. Salads are an easy option as they can be prepared in advance and, if you include one made with potatoes, pasta, rice or other grains, you won't have to worry about cooking any accompaniments on the day.

That said, if there is room on the barbecue grill, it is fun to include vegetable parcels, chargrilled corn cobs or crisp potato skins. Ever popular, garlic bread is a convenient compromise as, once prepared, all it requires is gentle warming on the side of the grill.

Home-made dressings and sauces are more flavoursome, economical and often healthier than ready-made. It's good to offer a choice but to save yourself too much work, bear in mind that some will double up. Hummus, for example, is lovely with summer vegetables and also a perfect accompaniment to lamb, guacamole is the ideal partner for steak, kebabs and chargrilled vegetables, while a spicy barbecue sauce is equally good with sausages, burgers and chops.

Try to ensure that side dishes, especially any like coleslaw, made with mayonnaise, are placed in the shade. Don't forget a supply of serving spoons.

corn on the cob

ingredients

SERVES 4

4 corn cobs, with husks

herb butter

100 g/3¹/₂ oz butter

1 tbsp chopped fresh parsley

1 tsp chopped fresh chives

1 tsp chopped fresh thyme

grated rind of 1 lemon

salt and pepper

method

1 Preheat the barbecue. To prepare the corn cobs, peel back the husks and remove the silken hairs. Fold back the husks and secure them in place with string if necessary.

2 Blanch the corn cobs in a large saucepan of boiling water for 5 minutes. Remove the corn cobs with a slotted spoon and drain thoroughly. Cook the corn cobs over medium–hot coals for 20–30 minutes, turning frequently.

3 Meanwhile, soften the butter and beat in the parsley, chives, thyme, lemon rind and salt and pepper to taste. Transfer the corn cobs to serving plates, remove the string and pull back the husks. Serve each with a generous portion of herb butter.

courgette & cheese parcels

ingredients

SERVES 2

1 small bunch of fresh mint

2 large courgettes

1 tbsp olive oil, plus extra
for brushing

115 g/4 oz feta cheese,
cut into strips

pepper

method

1 Preheat the barbecue. Using a sharp knife, finely chop enough mint to fill 1 tablespoon. Reserve until required. Cut out 2 rectangles of foil, each large enough to enclose a courgette, and brush lightly with olive oil. Cut a few slits along the length of each courgette and place them on the foil rectangles.

2 Insert strips of feta cheese along the slits in the courgettes, then drizzle the olive oil over the top, sprinkle with the reserved chopped mint and season to taste with pepper. Fold in the sides of the foil rectangles securely and seal the edges to enclose the cheese-stuffed courgettes completely.

3 Bake the courgette parcels in the barbecue embers for 30–40 minutes. Carefully unwrap the parcels and serve immediately.

stuffed mushrooms

ingredients

SERVES 12

12 open-cap mushrooms
4 tsp olive oil
4 spring onions, chopped
100 g/3$\frac{1}{2}$ oz fresh brown
    breadcrumbs
1 tsp chopped fresh oregano
100 g/3$\frac{1}{2}$ oz feta cheese
    or chorizo sausage
sunflower oil, for oiling

method

1 Preheat the barbecue. Remove the stalks from the mushrooms and chop the stalks finely. Heat half of the olive oil in a large frying pan. Add the mushroom stalks and spring onions and sauté briefly.

2 Mix the mushroom stalks and spring onions together in a large bowl. Add the breadcrumbs and oregano to the mushrooms and spring onions, mix well, then reserve until required.

3 If you are using feta, crumble the cheese into small pieces in a small bowl. If you are using chorizo sausage, remove the skin and chop the flesh finely.

4 Add the crumbled feta cheese or chopped chorizo to the breadcrumb mixture and mix well. Spoon the stuffing mixture into the mushroom caps.

5 Drizzle the remaining olive oil over the stuffed mushrooms, then cook on an oiled rack over medium–hot coals for 8–10 minutes. Transfer the mushrooms to individual serving plates and serve while still hot.

stuffed tomato parcels

ingredients

SERVES 4

1 tbsp olive oil

2 tbsp sunflower seeds

1 onion, finely chopped

1 garlic clove, finely chopped

500 g/1 lb 2 oz fresh spinach,
    thick stalks removed and
    leaves shredded

pinch of freshly grated
    nutmeg

4 beef tomatoes

140 g/5 oz mozzarella
    cheese, diced

salt and pepper

method

1 Preheat the barbecue. Heat the oil in a heavy-based saucepan. Add the sunflower seeds and cook, stirring constantly, for 2 minutes, or until golden. Add the onion and cook over a low heat, stirring occasionally, for 5 minutes, or until softened but not browned. Add the garlic and spinach, cover and cook for 2–3 minutes, or until the spinach has wilted. Remove the saucepan from the heat and season to taste with nutmeg, salt and pepper. Leave to cool.

2 Using a sharp knife, cut off and reserve a thin slice from the top of each tomato and scoop out the flesh with a teaspoon, taking care not to pierce the shell. Chop the flesh and stir it into the spinach mixture with the mozzarella cheese.

3 Fill the tomato shells with the spinach and cheese mixture and replace the tops. Cut 4 squares of foil, each large enough to enclose a tomato. Place one tomato in the centre of each square and fold up the sides to enclose securely. Cook over hot coals, turning occasionally, for 10 minutes. Serve immediately in the foil parcels.

potato fans

ingredients

SERVES 6

6 large potatoes, scrubbed
  but not peeled
1 garlic clove, finely chopped
2 tbsp olive oil
salt and pepper

method

1 Preheat the barbecue. Using a sharp knife, make a series of cuts across the potatoes almost all the way through. Cut out 6 squares of foil, each large enough to enclose a potato, and place a potato on top of each one.

2 Mix together the garlic and olive oil and brush generously over the potatoes. Season with salt and pepper to taste. Fold up the sides of the foil to enclose the potatoes completely.

3 Cook over hot coals, turning occasionally, for 1 hour. To serve, open the foil parcels and gently pinch the potatoes to open up the fans.

crispy potato skins

ingredients

SERVES 4–6

8 small baking potatoes, scrubbed

50 g/1³/₄ oz butter, melted

salt and pepper

topping

6 spring onions, sliced

50 g/1³/₄ oz grated Gruyère cheese

50 g/1³/₄ oz salami, cut in to thin strips

method

1 Preheat the oven to 200°C/400°F/Gas Mark 6. Prick the potatoes with a fork and bake for 1 hour, or until tender. Alternatively, cook in a microwave on High for 12–15 minutes. Cut the potatoes in half and scoop out the flesh, leaving about 5 mm/¹/₄ inch potato flesh lining the skin.

2 Preheat the barbecue. Brush the insides of the potato with melted butter.

3 Place the skins, cut-side down, over medium–hot coals and cook for 10–15 minutes. Turn the potato skins over and barbecue for a further 5 minutes, or until they are crispy. Take care that they do not burn. Season the potato skins with salt and pepper to taste and serve while they are still warm.

4 If wished, the skins can be filled with a variety of toppings. Barbecue the potato skins as above for 10 minutes, then turn cut-side up and sprinkle with slices of spring onion, grated cheese and chopped salami. Barbecue for a further 5 minutes, or until the cheese begins to melt. Serve hot.

potato salad

ingredients

SERVES 4

700 g/1 lb 9 oz tiny new
    potatoes

8 spring onions

1 hard-boiled egg (optional)

250 ml/9 fl oz mayonnaise

1 tsp paprika

salt and pepper

2 tbsp snipped fresh chives,
    to garnish

pinch of paprika, to garnish

method

1 Bring a large saucepan of lightly salted water to the boil. Add the potatoes and cook for 10–15 minutes, or until they are just tender.

2 Drain the potatoes and rinse them under cold running water until completely cold. Drain again. Transfer the potatoes to a bowl and reserve until required. Using a sharp knife, slice the spring onions thinly on the diagonal. Chop the hard-boiled egg, if using.

3 Mix the mayonnaise, paprika and salt and pepper to taste together in a bowl. Pour the mixture over the potatoes. Add the spring onions and egg, if using, to the potatoes and toss together.

4 Transfer the potato salad to a serving bowl, sprinkle with snipped chives and a pinch of paprika. Cover and leave to chill in the refrigerator until required.

garlic bread

ingredients

SERVES 6

150 g/5^1/$_2$ oz butter, softened

3 cloves garlic, crushed

2 tbsp chopped fresh parsley

pepper

1 large or 2 small sticks of
    French bread

method

1 Mix together the butter, garlic and parsley in a bowl until well combined. Season with pepper to taste and mix well.

2 Cut a few lengthwise slits in the French bread. Spread the flavoured butter inside the slits and place the bread on a large sheet of thick kitchen foil.

3 Preheat the barbecue. Wrap the bread well in the foil and barbecue over hot coals for 10–15 minutes until the butter melts and the bread is piping hot.

4 Serve as an accompaniment to a wide range of dishes.

panzanella

ingredients

SERVES 4–6

250 g/9 oz stale focaccia,
ciabatta or French bread

4 large, vine-ripened
tomatoes

about 6 tbsp extra virgin olive
oil

4 red, yellow and/or orange
peppers

100 g/3¹/2 oz cucumber

1 large red onion, finely
chopped

8 canned anchovy fillets,
drained and chopped

2 tbsp capers in brine, rinsed
and patted dry

about 4 tbsp red wine vinegar

about 2 tbsp best-quality
balsamic vinegar

salt and pepper

fresh basil leaves, to garnish

method

1 Cut the bread into 2.5-cm/1-inch cubes
and place in a large bowl. Working over a
plate to catch any juices, quarter the tomatoes;
reserve the juices. Using a teaspoon, scoop
out the cores and seeds and discard, then
finely chop the flesh. Add to the bread cubes.

2 Drizzle 5 tablespoons of the olive oil over the
mixture and toss with your hands until well
coated. Pour in the reserved tomato juice and
toss again. Set aside for about 30 minutes.

3 Meanwhile, cut the peppers in half and
remove the cores and seeds. Place on a grill
rack under a preheated hot grill and grill for
10 minutes, or until the skins are charred and
the flesh softened. Place in a plastic bag,
seal and set aside for 20 minutes to allow the
steam to loosen the skins. Remove the skins,
then finely chop.

4 Cut the cucumber in half lengthways, then
cut each half into 3 strips lengthways. Using
a teaspoon, scoop out and discard the seeds.
Dice the cucumber.

5 Add the onion, peppers, cucumber, anchovy
fillets and capers to the bread and toss together.
Sprinkle with the red wine and balsamic
vinegars and season to taste with salt and
pepper. Drizzle with extra olive oil or vinegar
if necessary, but be cautious that it does not
become too greasy or soggy. Sprinkle the fresh
basil leaves over the salad and serve at once.

chargrilled vegetables with creamy pesto

ingredients

SERVES 4

1 red onion

1 fennel bulb

4 baby aubergines

4 baby courgettes

1 orange pepper

1 red pepper

2 beef tomatoes

2 tbsp olive oil

salt and pepper

1 fresh basil sprig, to garnish

creamy pesto

55 g/2 oz fresh basil leaves

15 g/^{1}/$_2$ oz pine kernels

1 garlic clove

pinch of coarse sea salt

25 g/1 oz freshly grated
   Parmesan cheese

50 ml/2 fl oz extra virgin olive
   oil

150 ml/5 fl oz natural Greek
   yogurt

method

1 Preheat the barbecue. To make the creamy pesto, place the basil, pine kernels, garlic and sea salt in a mortar and pound to a paste with a pestle. Gradually work in the Parmesan cheese, then gradually stir in the oil.

2 Place the yogurt in a small serving bowl and stir in 3–4 tablespoons of the pesto mixture. Cover with clingfilm and leave to chill in the refrigerator until required. Store any leftover pesto mixture in a screw-top jar in the refrigerator.

3 Prepare the vegetables. Cut the onion and fennel bulb into wedges, trim and slice the aubergines and courgettes, deseed and thickly slice the peppers and cut the tomatoes in half. Brush the vegetables with oil and season to taste with salt and pepper.

4 Cook the aubergines and peppers over hot coals for 3 minutes, then add the courgettes, onion, fennel and tomatoes and cook, turning occasionally and brushing with more oil if necessary, for a further 5 minutes. Transfer to a large serving plate and serve immediately with the pesto, garnished with a basil sprig.

summer vegetable parcels

ingredients

SERVES 4

1 kg/2 lb 4 oz mixed baby
    vegetables, such as
    carrots, asparagus, corn
    cobs, plum tomatoes,
    leeks, courgettes, chillies
    and onions

1 lemon

115 g/4 oz unsalted butter

3 tbsp chopped mixed fresh
    herbs, such as parsley,
    thyme, chives and chervil

2 garlic cloves

salt and pepper

method

1 Preheat the barbecue. Cut out 4 x 30-cm/
12-inch squares of foil and divide the
vegetables equally among them.

2 Using a grater, finely grate the lemon rind,
then squeeze the juice from the lemon and
reserve until required. Put the lemon rind,
butter, herbs and garlic into a food processor
and process until blended, then season to taste
with salt and pepper. Alternatively, beat
together in a bowl until blended.

3 Divide the butter equally among the vegetable
parcels, dotting it on top. Fold up the sides of
the foil to enclose the vegetables, sealing
securely. Cook over medium–hot coals, turning
occasionally, for 25–30 minutes. Open the
parcels, sprinkle with the reserved lemon juice
and serve immediately.

pasta salad with basil vinaigrette

ingredients

SERVES 4

225 g/8 oz dried fusilli

4 tomatoes

50 g/1¾ oz black olives

25 g/1 oz sun-dried
    tomatoes in oil

2 tbsp pine kernels

2 tbsp freshly grated
    Parmesan cheese

fresh basil leaves, to garnish

vinaigrette

15 g/½ oz basil leaves

1 garlic clove, crushed

2 tbsp freshly grated
    Parmesan cheese

4 tbsp extra virgin olive oil

2 tbsp lemon juice

salt and pepper

method

1 Cook the pasta in a large saucepan of lightly salted boiling water for 10–12 minutes, or until just tender but still firm to the bite. Drain the pasta, rinse under cold running water, then drain again thoroughly. Place the pasta in a large bowl.

2 Preheat the grill to medium. To make the vinaigrette, place the basil leaves, garlic, cheese, olive oil and lemon juice in a food processor. Season to taste with salt and pepper and process until the leaves are well chopped and the ingredients are combined. Alternatively, finely chop the basil leaves by hand and combine with the other vinaigrette ingredients. Pour the vinaigrette over the pasta and toss to coat.

3 Cut the tomatoes into wedges. Stone and halve the olives. Slice the sun-dried tomatoes. Toast the pine kernels on a baking tray under the hot grill until golden.

4 Add the tomatoes (fresh and sun-dried) and the olives to the pasta and mix until combined. Transfer the pasta mixture to a serving dish, sprinkle over the Parmesan and toasted pine kernels and serve garnished with a few basil leaves.

tropical rice salad

ingredient

SERVES 4

115 g/4 oz long-grain rice

4 spring onions

225 g/8 oz canned pineapple
  pieces in natural juice

200 g/7 oz canned
  sweetcorn, drained

2 red peppers, deseeded
  and diced

3 tbsp sultanas

salt and pepper

dressing

1 tbsp groundnut oil

1 tbsp hazelnut oil

1 tbsp light soy sauce

1 garlic clove, finely chopped

1 tsp chopped fresh ginger

method

1 Cook the rice in a large saucepan of lightly
salted boiling water for 15 minutes, or until
tender. Drain thoroughly and rinse under
cold running water. Place the rice in a large
serving bowl.

2 Using a sharp knife, finely chop the spring
onions. Drain the pineapple pieces, reserving
the juice in a jug. Add the pineapple pieces,
sweetcorn, red peppers, chopped spring
onions and sultanas to the rice and mix lightly.

3 Add all the dressing ingredients to the
reserved pineapple juice, whisking well, and
season to taste with salt and pepper. Pour the
dressing over the salad and toss until the
salad is thoroughly coated. Serve immediately.

green bean & feta salad

ingredients

SERVES 4

350 g/12 oz green beans, trimmed

1 red onion, chopped

3–4 tbsp chopped fresh coriander

2 radishes, thinly sliced

75 g/2¾ oz feta cheese, crumbled

1 tsp chopped fresh oregano or ½ tsp dried oregano

2 tbsp red wine vinegar or fruit vinegar

5 tbsp extra virgin olive oil

6 ripe cherry or small tomatoes, quartered

pepper

method

1 Bring about 5 cm/2 inches of water to the boil in the base of a steamer or in a medium saucepan. Add the green beans to the top of the steamer or place them in a metal colander set over the pan of water. Cover and steam for about 5 minutes until just tender.

2 Transfer the beans to a bowl and add the onion, coriander, radishes and feta cheese.

3 Sprinkle the oregano over the salad, then grind pepper over to taste. Whisk the vinegar and olive oil together and then pour over the salad. Toss gently to mix well.

4 Transfer to a serving platter, surround with the tomato quarters and serve at once or chill until ready to serve.

tabbouleh

ingredients

SERVES 4

175 g/6 oz bulgar wheat

3 tbsp extra virgin olive oil

4 tbsp lemon juice

4 spring onions

1 green pepper, deseeded
    and sliced

4 tomatoes, chopped

2 tbsp chopped fresh parsley

2 tbsp chopped fresh mint

8 black olives, stoned

salt and pepper

fresh mint sprigs, to garnish

method

1 Place the bulgar wheat in a large bowl and add enough cold water to cover. Leave to stand for 30 minutes, or until the wheat has doubled in size. Drain well and press out as much liquid as possible. Spread out the wheat on kitchen paper to dry.

2 Place the wheat in a serving bowl. Mix the olive oil and lemon juice together in a jug and season to taste with salt and pepper. Pour the lemon mixture over the wheat and leave to marinate for 1 hour.

3 Using a sharp knife, finely chop the spring onions, then add to the salad with the green pepper, tomatoes, parsley and mint and toss lightly to mix. Top the salad with the olives and garnish with fresh mint sprigs, then serve.

home-made tomato sauce

ingredients

SERVES 4

1 tbsp butter

2 tbsp olive oil

1 onion, chopped

1 garlic clove, finely chopped

400 g/14 oz canned tomatoes
or 450 g/1 lb fresh
tomatoes, peeled

1 tbsp tomato purée

100 ml/3^1/$_2$ fl oz red wine

150 ml/5 fl oz vegetable stock

^{1}/$_2$ tsp sugar

1 bay leaf

salt and pepper

method

1 Melt the butter with the oil in a large saucepan over a medium heat, add the onion and garlic and cook, stirring frequently, for 5 minutes, or until the onion has softened and is beginning to brown.

2 Add all the remaining ingredients to the saucepan and season to taste with salt and pepper. Bring to the boil, then reduce the heat to low and leave to simmer, uncovered and stirring occasionally, for 30 minutes, or until the sauce has thickened.

3 Remove and discard the bay leaf, pour the sauce into a food processor or blender and process until smooth. Alternatively, using the back of a wooden spoon, push the sauce through a nylon sieve into a bowl.

4 If serving immediately, reheat the sauce gently in a pan. Alternatively, store and reheat before serving.

spicy barbecue sauce

ingredients

SERVES 4

2 tbsp sunflower oil

1 large onion, chopped

2 garlic cloves, chopped

225 g/8 oz canned chopped
    tomatoes

1 tbsp Worcestershire sauce

2 tbsp brown fruity sauce

2 tbsp light muscovado sugar

4 tbsp white wine vinegar

$1/2$ tsp mild chilli powder

$1/4$ tsp mustard powder

dash of Tabasco sauce

salt and pepper

cooked sausages or burger in
    bread rolls, to serve

method

1 Preheat the barbecue. To make the sauce, heat the oil in a saucepan and fry the onion and garlic for 4–5 minutes, until softened and just beginning to brown.

2 Add the tomatoes, Worcestershire sauce, brown fruity sauce, sugar, white wine vinegar, chilli powder, mustard powder and Tabasco sauce to the saucepan. Add salt and pepper to taste, and bring to the boil.

3 Reduce the heat and simmer gently for 10–15 minutes, until the sauce begins to thicken slightly, stirring occasionally. Set aside and keep warm until required. Serve with cooked sausages or burgers.

coleslaw

ingredients

SERVES 10–12

150 ml/5 fl oz mayonnaise

150 ml/5 fl oz low-fat natural
    yogurt

dash of Tabasco sauce

1 medium head white
    cabbage

4 carrots

1 green pepper

salt and pepper

method

1 To make the dressing, mix the mayonnaise, yogurt, Tabasco sauce and salt and pepper to taste together in a small bowl. Chill in the refrigerator until required.

2 Cut the cabbage in half and then into quarters. Remove and discard the tough centre stalk. Shred the cabbage leaves finely. Wash the leaves under cold running water and dry thoroughly on kitchen paper. Peel the carrots and shred in a food processor or on a mandolin. Alternatively, roughly grate the carrot. Quarter and deseed the pepper and cut the flesh into thin strips.

3 Mix the vegetables together in a large serving bowl and toss to mix. Pour over the dressing and toss until the vegetables are well coated. Cover and chill until required.

mayonnaise

ingredients

SERVES 2–4

2 large egg yolks

2 tsp Dijon mustard

$^3/_4$ tsp salt, or to taste

white pepper

2 tbsp lemon juice or white wine vinegar

about 300 ml/10 fl oz sunflower oil

method

1 Whizz the egg yolks with the Dijon mustard, salt and white pepper to taste in a food processor, blender or by hand. Add the lemon juice and whizz again.

2 With the motor still running or still beating, add the oil, drop by drop at first. When the sauce begins to thicken, the oil can then be added in a slow, steady stream. Taste and adjust the seasoning with extra salt, pepper and lemon juice if necessary. If the sauce seems too thick, slowly add 1 tablespoon hot water, single cream or lemon juice.

3 Use at once or store in an airtight container in the refrigerator for up to 1 week.

tzatziki

ingredients

SERVES 4

1 small cucumber

300 ml/10 fl oz authentic
   Greek yogurt

1 large garlic clove, crushed

1 tbsp chopped fresh mint
   or dill

salt and pepper

warm pitta bread, to serve

method

1 Peel, then coarsely grate the cucumber. Put in a sieve and squeeze out as much of the water as possible. Put the cucumber into a bowl.

2 Add the yogurt, garlic and chopped mint (reserve a little as a garnish, if liked) to the cucumber and season with pepper. Mix well together and chill in the fridge for about 2 hours before serving.

3 To serve, stir the cucumber and yogurt dip and transfer to a serving bowl. Sprinkle with salt and accompany with warmed pitta bread.

aïoli

ingredients

SERVES 2–4

3 large garlic cloves, finely
    chopped

2 egg yolks

225 ml/8 fl oz extra virgin
    olive oil

1 tbsp lemon juice

1 tbsp lime juice

1 tbsp Dijon mustard

1 tbsp chopped fresh
    tarragon

salt and pepper

1 fresh tarragon sprig,
    to garnish

method

1 Ensure that all the ingredients are at room temperature. Place the garlic and egg yolks in a food processor and process until well blended. With the motor running, pour in the oil teaspoon by teaspoon through the feeder tube until the mixture starts to thicken, then pour in the remaining oil in a thin stream until a thick mayonnaise forms.

2 Add the lemon and lime juices, mustard and tarragon and season to taste with salt and pepper. Blend until smooth, then transfer to a non-metallic bowl. Garnish with a tarragon sprig.

3 Use at once or store in an airtight container in the refrigerator for up to 1 week.

hummus

ingredients

SERVES 8

225 g/8 oz chickpeas,
    covered with water and
    soaked overnight
juice of 2 large lemons
150 ml/5 fl oz tahini paste
2 garlic cloves, crushed
4 tbsp extra virgin olive oil
small pinch of ground cumin
salt and pepper
pitta bread, to serve

to garnish
1 tsp paprika
chopped flat-leaf parsley

method

1 Drain the chickpeas, put in a saucepan and cover with cold water. Bring to the boil then simmer for about 2 hours, until very tender.

2 Drain the chickpeas, reserving a little of the liquid, and put in a food processor, reserving a few to garnish. Blend the chickpeas until smooth, gradually adding the lemon juice and enough reserved liquid to form a smooth, thick purée. Add the tahini paste, garlic, 3 tablespoons of the olive oil and the cumin and blend until smooth. Season with salt and pepper.

3 Turn the mixture into a shallow serving dish and chill in the fridge for 2–3 hours before serving. To serve, mix the reserved olive oil with the paprika and drizzle over the top of the dish. Sprinkle with the parsley and the reserved chickpeas. Accompany with warm pitta bread.

guacamole

ingredients

SERVES 4

2 large, ripe avocados

juice of 1 lime, or to taste

2 tsp olive oil

$1/2$ onion, finely chopped

1 fresh green chilli, such as
    poblano, deseeded and
    finely chopped

1 garlic clove, crushed

$1/4$ tsp ground cumin

1 tbsp chopped fresh
    coriander

salt and pepper

tortilla chips, to serve

fresh dill or coriander sprigs,
    to garnish

method

1 Cut the avocados in half lengthways and twist the 2 halves in opposite directions to separate. Stab the stone with the point of a sharp knife and lift out.

2 Peel, then roughly chop the avocado halves and place in a non-metallic bowl. Squeeze over the lime juice and add the oil. Mash the avocados with a fork until the desired consistency is achieved – either chunky or smooth. Blend in the onion, chilli, garlic, cumin and chopped coriander, then season to taste with salt and pepper.

3 Transfer to a serving dish and serve immediately, to avoid discoloration, with tortilla chips and garnished with fresh dill sprigs.

tomato salsa

ingredients

SERVES 6

450 g/1 lb firm, ripe tomatoes

1 fresh jalapeño or other
   small hot chilli pepper

2 tsp extra virgin olive oil

1 garlic clove, crushed

grated rind and juice of 1 lime

pinch of sugar

4 tbsp chopped fresh
   coriander

salt

fresh coriander sprigs,
   to garnish

method

1 Using a sharp knife, finely dice the tomatoes and put into a bowl with the seeds. Halve the chilli, remove and discard the seeds and very finely dice the flesh. Add to the tomatoes.

2 Add all the remaining ingredients to the tomatoes, season to taste with salt and mix well together.

3 Turn the mixture into a small, non-metallic serving bowl, cover and leave at room temperature for 30 minutes to allow the flavours to combine. If not serving straight away, the salsa can be stored in the refrigerator for up to 2–3 days, but it is best if allowed to return to room temperature for 1 hour before serving. Serve garnished with fresh coriander sprigs.